Resident Alien

Kazim Ali

Resident Alien

ON BORDER-CROSSING AND THE
UNDOCUMENTED DIVINE

UNIVERSITY OF MICHIGAN PRESS

Ann Arbor

Published in the United States of America by
The University of Michigan Press
Manufactured in the United States of America
⊗ Printed on acid-free paper

2018   2017   2016   2015   4   3   2   1

A CIP catalog record for this book is available from the British Library.
ISBN 978-0-472-07291-0 (hardcover : alk. paper)
ISBN 978-0-472-05291-2 (pbk. : alk. paper)
ISBN 978-0-472-12147-2 (e-book)

Contents

Acknowledgments

Some essays appeared previously in earlier forms in the following magazines and journals:

American Poetry Review: "Poetry and Place"
Asian American Literary Review: "September 14"
Catamaran: "Yoga and the Cessation of the Self"
English Language Notes: "The Opening"
FIELD: "Attempted Treasons"
Harvard Divinity Bulletin: "Acts of Faith"
Mary: "Interview with Nima Najafi-Kianfar"
Poetry Society of America: "What's American About American Poetry?" and "Old School"
Squaw Review: "Ode to Silence"
Superstition: "Disappearances"

And in the following books:

"Doubting and Seeking" in *A God in the House: Poets Talk About Faith*, edited by Ilya Kaminsky and Katherine Towles, Tupelo Press.

"Bringing the House Down" in *Anne Carson: Ecstatic Lyre*, edited by Joshua Marie Wilkinson, University of Michigan Press.

"The Rose is My Qibla" in *Water's Footfall* by Sohrab Sepehri, translated by Kazim Ali with Mohammad Jafar Mahallati, Omnidawn Publishing.

"Poets Crossing Borders" in *Strangest of Theaters*, edited by Brian Turner and Susan Rich, MacSweeney's Publishing/Poetry Foundation.

I thank Nima Najafi-Kianfar, Ilya Kaminsky and Britney Gulbrandsen for asking me difficult questions.

Parag Khandhar, Lawrence-Minh Bui Davis, Gerald Maa, Susan McGarrity, Elizabeth Robinson, Jennifer Phelps, Katharine Towles, Elizabeth Scanlon, Shona Romaya, Brett Fletcher Lauer, Jared Hawkley, Brian Turner, Susan Rich, David Young, David Walker, Joshua Marie Wilkinson, Julie Carr, Susan Zemka, Karen An-Wei Lee and Charif Shanahan are the editors who asked me to write pieces for them and so occasioned this book into being.

Many years ago Brett Hall Jones, Lisa Alvarez and the Squaw Valley Community of Writers created a space for me in which the poet inside learned to breathe. Robert Hass ushered me back into that sacred valley. I am more grateful than I can properly say. My "Ode to Silence" is dedicated to Oakley and Barbara Hall who made and make a place where holy beings learn their true natures.

Friends, colleagues and students at Oberlin College and around the world make it easy to think all the time. It is hard to properly thank anyone but this time I will single out Ben Jones and Tanya Rosen-Jones, Jennifer Karmin, Amy Antongiovanni, Eric Estes, Jed Deppman, Bonnie Cheng, Sandhya Subramanian, Ian Rhodewalt, Sridala Swami, Navid Pourghazi, Blas Falconer, Paris Gravley, and Erin Gravley.

I must always thank my yoga teachers, this time Emily Paxhia, Justin Glanville, Tim Floreen, Amanda Moran, Chris Otchy and Terri Lewis.

I thank, each time and always, Marco Wilkinson.

Part 1

September Fourteenth

SUTURE: a thread sewing two ends of a wound together. From the ancient Sanskrit word *sutra*, thread. All sources of wisdom that descend into the depths.

FATHOM: to understand the dark deep reaches. From a nautical measurement ascertained by dropping a weighted thread down into the water.

I'm threaded to time, a day ten years ago, cold Tuesday morning, stone-blue sky yet unsundered.

Early August 2001 I moved north of the city into the Hudson Valley to teach at the Culinary Institute of America. There I learned yoga, how the body stretches, how to breathe.

Late August 2001, driving home one Saturday night at around three in the morning I had to pull over on the side of route 9, staring skywards.

A thousand harrowing lights streaking across the sky. As I read the night's incandescent sentences aloud I forgot: these are not objects passing far above, rather they are objects caught in the orbit of the Earth.

Falling out of the sky. Toward me.

Who brought fire from the sky first? What streaks angry toward me through the history of the cosmos? Newton's second law: every action has an equal and opposite reaction—does it apply to humans?

To use the vocabulary of angry children, we *kill each other to death.*

What's after? We drew the war on the slabs of the street, we whispered it into Ever. We timed our lives against its length. Our death-vane, our anchor.

Odysseus took ten years to travel home from a ten-year war. It takes a long time to back away from a city still burning.
And what do we fathom about war, those of us who stay home?

The sky above New York City in September of 2001 looked nothing so much to me as the sky above Baghdad in January of 1991. And the Hudson River, on which I lived at the time, is a river that returns to its source.

Jean Baudrillard famously said the Gulf War "did not take place." He didn't mean it didn't *happen*—because of course it did; the hundreds of thousands of dead Iraqi civilians advance moaning in the Underworld to howl their deaths backward in time to the moment our hero Odysseus visits, seeking Teiresias, the transgendered prophet.

Baudrillard meant it had broken all the rules of how we had understood "war" up until that point. Fought by remote control, fought undeclared, divorced from any social significance in our quotidian lives.

And so when war came screaming down out of the sky to visit us our first reaction was fear but then so quickly rage.

So sing muse the rage of America that sent countless souls of young women howling out their resentment to the dark house of Hades.

Of course when Euripides did the radical and unthinkable thing—setting a play called *The Trojan Women* in the prison-of-war camps before the burning city of Troy—he made our hero Odysseus into a complicit oppressor at best, a thug and bully at worst.

4

"Every war that begins has long since begun in the hearts of the people," Mark Twain said. And true to form when the door of fire opened we walked through.

And is the thought of trying to make peace in a time of endless war so foreign like the mixing of oil and water?

After all at the beginning of *The Iliad,* every last soldier, every Trojan, every Greek, *wants* the war to be over, but no one has the courage or vision to manage it.

So undone the thunder, I want to know now how can we return ourselves, how to speak the right riddles backwards, unwind the years of rage and war.

Time swiftly passes. Unlike the Hudson, most rivers spill only one way: from source to sea.

But doesn't the water spill back a thousand ways or more? Won't it yet evaporate into the air, be reborn as clouds, rain themselves down—

To dream against war is to be alive, to be like the water which always changes forms.

To embrace the war is to be like fire, to consume everything, to burn until suffocated or until there is no matter left solid to feed on.

I choose as I chose on September 12th, 2001, to look now for opportunities for peace, to understand the political and material conditions of the last century or more that led us to this place, to hope to be able to untangle the imperial knots of history in hopes of weaving a peaceful and peace-filled future.

I promised it while the stones were falling from the sky a month before any planes flew into the buildings, I promised it again that morning, watching the buildings fall.

On Friday September 14th, 2001, I stood in front of my class and the students were quiet. Shall we continue talking about emulsified sauces, or do you want to talk about what has happened in New York City?

Emulsified sauces, they begged, not wanting to face any more, at least not for the next fifty minutes. I was grateful. Looking with tenderness and understanding at their frightened faces, their crisp white chef's jackets.

In an emulsified sauce oil and water can indeed mix, provided the barriers between cells are so gently and subtly broken down. The emulsion of water into oil makes the combination even thicker and stronger than before.

At the end of the epic *The Odyssey* the men of Odysseus and the men of the suitors' families are charging at each other, the air thick with spears and war cries. Suddenly Athena, in the voice of Mentor, cries out something like, "All right, enough is enough, everyone settle down!"

And mysteriously—or perhaps not—everyone does. Perhaps peace was the truest dream in their hearts, one they didn't have the stomach to express.

Acts of Faith

This past summer I went to Israel and Palestine. Though the main reason I went was to learn more about what American tax dollars support there and to meet Israeli and Palestinian activists of all faiths—who were working on non-violent solutions—another more secret reason I went was to see the landscapes so beautifully written about by Darwish. I found them. I found Darwish too—I visited his body interred in the hills above Ramallah, and later I visited the now bramble-covered ruins of his hometown of Birweh, one of the villages destroyed in the 1948 war; all that remains is a ruined cemetery and the remnants of what was once a church. I also found the likeness of Darwish himself, painted with loving care, life-sized, on a side-street off of Rukab Street in Ramallah.

So which of the four places does the spirit of the poet really live—in the haunted rubble of the village, in the actual dirt of the grave, marked on the wall of the city, or in the abstract of the landscape itself. Or is the only resting place for the poet now in his poems and books, scattered—like he was—across the wide world.

Some Muslims believe that you can use books—the Quran specifically—for divination. You dream of your problem and then open the book and the verse you open to will tell you what you need. When, after ten years of a friend begging me to read Robert Duncan, I first opened a book of his poems, I opened it to this line: "What songs my mother taught me. Not to sing."[1]

My mother taught me many songs, including poems and Muslim prayers, mostly in Arabic but sometimes in Urdu and once in a while in English. I have a hard time explaining what my relation to religion and spirituality is, not because I am not sure if I believe or not but because "belief" for me is—has always been—a dynamic network of thoughts feeding one into the other moving backward and forward and sideways. I can't ask a question because then there will be an answer and where does that lead you?

The other reason I can't settle on a relationship with god is because I am not sure what the analogy between body and spirit or the existent world and the so-called "afterlife" (though maybe "other-life" would be more accurate?) really is. Maybe this is at least in part due to what my physical body itself learned about gender and physical responses to the bodies around it. In other words even as a young boy I had no interest in what young boys were *supposed* to be like and then as a young man I knew my body was not a heteronormative body; desire for human love and desire for connection with god seemed, at least according to the teachings I received, to exclude one another. And I was not about to be caught between my self and my Self. I knew this a long time before I had either vocabulary or inclination to explain it.

And what were the songs—within my own body but also within the air and space and water of the world—that I had been taught *not* to sing?

So it took me a long time to learn how to sing and a long time more before I really could talk to God beyond mere ventroliquism—the prayers I and others have been taught to repeat, syllable for syllable, hoping to breathe our own individual desires into them.

When I was in Israel I had the fortune of meeting poet Rivka Miriam. Miriam told me about two different trips she had taken to India. On the first trip she fell in love with Indian spirituality and the concept of god as part of every moment of the day and every piece of matter in the world. She loved that each human held a piece of god and that our life was a long task of trying to take the piece back for a reunion. On her second trip the same concept made her despair. She realized that she loved the uniqueness of each human spirit, that it was our uniqueness that made us worthy of god in the first place, so what would it mean to surrender that? I am not sure the second experience is the answer to the first or the other way around. I think the whole story is the story of both trips together, the crux of blessed matter.

Anyhow, why pray at all? God is not going to answer you in words you can understand and depending on what you believe God may not be going to answer you at all. I think of prayer as being a verbal ritual to access or give shape to the divine formless and unstable energy not collected and coalesced into carnal form. If religion and ritual are meant to prepare one's own small body to truly access the further beyond it seems a rough and arbitrary operation.

After all, like poetry—*supposedly*—the language of prayer is important to the last syllable, isn't it? It *has to be* in Sanskrit, Arabic, Latin or whatever, doesn't it? We killed each other over the question, killed each other over translating sacred books, over mistranslating them, over mistreating them.

And if all the many tongues are roads inside, to the spirit or Spirit or whatever you prefer, then are we left with an anarchy of thought, a babble of contested words? Duncan goes on to say:[2]

> In the book of the birds he reads letters of an alphabet he
>   does not understand.
> [. . .]
> One of the words standing before Babel fell into tongues was
>   a bird there which was the sun there and he sounded as a
>   letter he could not read.

This is what I want to know—that there are mysteries in the world unknowable for us to use this lifetime to know. It is hard because so much knowledge has gone before and so many scriptures exist and in places like the United States, Israel, India, Iran and other places, people use these scriptures and the centuries of interpretation of them, to make laws, laws meant to govern the actions of human bodies. Laws that explain how to control them, manipulate and sometimes provide the justification, means and methods for punishing them and killing them.

If it is true that there are alphabets we don't understand, letters we cannot read, then I feel as if we have a shot at something new.

There are letters you cannot read scattered all through the Quran. They have no purpose for the lay reader; according to the commentators they are private coded messages meant for the prophet Muhammad himself. But it doesn't really make sense if you think about it—was it a private document for him alone or meant for all the believers? And to whose benefit would it be for us to merely be looking over his shoulder aware there was information we could never understand? The Quran, one can say with certainty, begs a reader to think about it. Begs over and over again in a repeated verse that goes, "Surely there are signs here for those of you that would think about it."

I like that: a book that has its own desires. It seems that we in our contemporary moment of scientific, poetic, erotic knowledge—teetering on the edge of disaster with the real possibility of planetary, spiritual and sexual death—have a chance to taste original knowledge, to move into an actually *new* understanding: of ourselves, of the universe itself. How *does* matter hold together and fly apart?

In which case, Babel—the multiplicity of tongues and scattering of nations—was not a curse or punishment for trying to reach God but maybe instead a pat on the back for good effort—it was a high tower after all. "But try *this* instead," a good teacher might say instead, stuffing a daffodil in one mouth, a chrysanthemum in another, a rose in the third.

When I was in India myself, a couple of years before I met Rivka Miriam, I felt similarly entranced. I told an audience in Hyderabad about seeing divine potential everywhere I went—to the Ganges River, to the great banyan tree at the Kolkata Botanical Gardens which is half a mile across, to the massive five-story high rocks pressed up out of the ancient volcano range under the Deccan Plateau. "It's a form of laziness," one of the critics there told me. "You Americans indulge in spirituality the way you shop at the supermarket—just picking things off the shelf."

And here's me with a marigold in my mouth.

It's hard enough to explain anything in ordinary speech but imagine trying to do something practical (like laying mortar or installing an arch) while speaking the language of flowers. Dana Levin, in "Letter to GC," says:[3]

> I would be disingenuous if I said "being understood" is not important to me.

Between the ceiling of private dream and the floor of public
    speech
Between the coin and the hand it crosses

God might be there, anyhow, lurking somewhere between
the public speech of bricklaying and the private whispering of a
poem. And if metaphor flies because it actually *fails* at accurate
description, then it would be similar to money that had no value-
equivalent, currency of a nation which doesn't exist.

Though even nations that do not exist can imagine them-
selves, sometimes concretely. In Haifa my friend Ian paid for
our lunch with his ATM card issued by the Bank of Palestine.

Coins—with their precise equivalences of denomination and
yield—are the exact opposite of the tenuous relationship be-
tween signifier and meaning implicit in poetry and god when
you never know what you mean when you write it and never re-
ally know what is meant when you read it. It's this drama Levin
might be writing to G. C. Waldrep about—this fear of not being
understood. She goes on to confess being "Adrift in the dark-
ness but readying oars" is "my kind of religion."

To be found, to be understood, to have our prayers heard—a
person will travel around the world if they think it will bring
them closer to God. Muslims go to Mecca, Jews may go to the
Western Wall, Christians might go to Rome or to Jerusalem. I
think my Pagan friend might have it easiest since all she has to
do is go outside. My friend Rachel Tzvia Back says one of the
Hebrew names of God is "the Place," in which case you ought to
be able to find Him anywhere, not just in a black stone or a rem-
nant of an old retaining wall, and in fact localizing that energy
to a single physical place may serve only to limit the boundless-
ness of that energy. "Don't pay so much attention to the jug,"
Rumi warns cheerfully, "that you forget to drink the water."

Rachel goes on, in her poem "Jerusalem Couplets," to say:[4]

A faith that asks
no questions, is fed

by loss.
Keeps its eyes

and ears closed
through the telling.

As I crossed and re-crossed the so-called Green Line which
divides East and West Jerusalem I became literally dizzy. That
city asks a new question every minute. Divided in half and then
with an old city divided in quarters, it is governed by a specific
set of written and unwritten rules about who has keys to which
door, who might walk where and which streets receive garbage
collection on which schedule and which name God is called by
at which hour of the day. It is hard to find god in a place of such
compartmentalizing but it is in everyone's best interests who live
there and who visit there to continue to try.

The Via Dolorosa wends its way from deep inside the Muslim
Quarter to the Church of the Holy Sepulcher. It was identified
as the route of Jesus on the day of the crucifixion by Helena, the
mother of Constantine, who had a dream about it. She might
have asked the olive trees in the garden at Gethsemane, at least
two of which have been dated back to the time of the ministry
of—as he was called then—Yeshua. Each station of the cross is
marked by a small metal tablet bearing a Roman numeral. Along
the route one passes souvenir shops, chapels, falafel stands, and
occasionally strands of barbed wire overhead, surveillance cam-
eras and Israeli flags; these mark so-called urban settlements,
places Jewish Israelis have rented or bought buildings in the
Muslim Quarter of the old city and moved in.

Of the contested rock at the heart of the summit called by
Muslims Al-Aqsa ("the Far Place") and by Jews the Temple
Mount, Back writes:[5]

The horse flew because the stone
on which he stood was wet.

Under red rugs the stone
still is damp.

The rock—you can't see much of it but you can climb down
inside into its heart—is said to be the place from which Prophet
Muhammad launched himself heavenward, the place Abraham

12

came to sacrifice his son Isaac, the place the Ark of the Covenant rested for a while, even said to be the place Adam and Eve entered the world from the Garden. If there's a piece of spiritual real estate to argue over, this is it.

But maybe if Rachel is right and God's name is "*the* Place," then a rock, a wall, a cathedral or oak tree are just that—objects, not holy; or at least not holy the way we think about it.

For pilgrims walking the stations of the cross—the literal places in Jerusalem or the metaphorical representations in churches around the world—(kissing each marker as they pass) at least the journey is *experiential,* interactive—

Michael Dickman writes about the first station of the cross in a series of poems called "Stations": [6]

> You have to listen carefully like dirt
> You have to fold back their wings with your wings
> Dig yourself out with your fingers
> Your teeth
> You're going to die anyway and not because it's natural but because
>   they want you to
> They hand you your death they say here it is

As a human body I guess I do have the privilege to be like dirt listening. And I know, because my partner is a farmer, that dirt is a breathing, living universe of organisms, a galaxy of richness unto itself. And it's the human that has to turn its back on the received knowledge of scripture, the whispering revelations of angelic beings, in order to find his own path to liberation—to dig his way out of his own grave.

It's a yogic course of action, but it's the heart of the story of the crucifixion too, isn't it? That God had to become human in order to attain liberation himself.

Dickman's poem talks about the cross as well:

> The little cross is somewhere in my room not doing
>   imitations of birds
> Not digging itself out
> Even though it has four points
> And can fly

It's not quite fair to leave the poet still in the ground, his mouth filled with dirt, scrabbling at the earth, and the cross in his room no help at all, but there are thirteen more stations in Dickman's poem and by the end of it, "The cross is so small that it can fit in the palm of my hand/It can fit in my brain/I didn't think there was room for it anymore on earth but there is room."[7]

Maybe why I drift from text to text, scripture to scripture, name of God to name of God is precisely not "spiritual laziness" but an idea that one should be "unhomed" from one's own body, or understanding or language—in Babel—in order to know anything at all. The Ganges at Varnasi is full of people who came to walk into the river, to experience the flow of its waters. I did not walk in but was rowed in a boat through the mist. The surface of the water was studded with floating marigold garlands, remnants of the Saraswati Puja which had taken place the night before. Occasionally a reed limb, the statue dismembered by the river, would float by.

The puja was nothing so much as crowds of young men, dancing into the streets to throbbing club-mixes of the goddess' mantra, pounding out from giant portable speakers strapped to cycle-rickshaws.

The sound was still thumping in my eardrums the next morning through the mist and chilly silence.

In my hand was a book by Meena Alexander. In between the pages of the book, crushed marigolds. Even today when I open that book flower fragments sprinkle out. In it I read:[8]

What will love do to us?
No one can answer this.

The moment of transformation can be a moment of fear. We want to live our lives, and sometimes this means holding on to certain ideas about ourselves. Knowledge, as it was in the story of the garden, is a frightening thing, can lead to disaster. We could, as Alexander writes, be "struck dumb by the burden of heaven."[9]

I was in the check-out line of a grocery store in Portland, Oregon, when someone behind me suddenly asked, "Are you Kazim Ali?" *Am I,* I wondered, for a fleeting moment turning and panicking. The questioner was a young man, a stockboy, his green apron wrapped around his waist, a crate of purple cabbages in his arms. And if I was this "Kazim Ali," was I the one he was thinking of?

When I fessed up to the crime he told me he was a poet and that his name was Andrew Michael Roberts. We talked for a short while and I left him, hurrying home with my Thai basil and coconut milk to prepare a curry for my hosts. But the next day at the bookstore, looking for a new book by Donald Revell, what should I see on the shelf but a small book by Andrew Michael Roberts. And I opened the book to the poem "What I Know of the Moon": [10]

> i am only half myself
> the other side's
> a dark idea
> i like to believe in

So what if it is true that I wander from idea to idea, from site to site, the river to the banyan, wondering if each place might have its own meaning, its own tongue, its own strange tune I was never taught to understand. If I have an attraction to the poetry of indeterminacy, disjunction, or fragment and conjecture it is not necessarily an aesthetic interest (though it is that too) it is because I believe the "self" is a risky conjecture itself, a weird coalition of celestial and spiritual matter (surely these are so different after all), a wobbly and wild thing that quivers through life the way a needle on an old-fashioned radio quivers at its frequency or the way a compass needle quivers as it searches for the "real" magnetic north, which a scientist will explain to you is a floating and not fixed point.

You are half yourself and the other part is just a set of notions—some of them brilliant, some of them ridiculous, but in any case you will have to think hard in order to sort yourself out and sometimes it will take a stranger in the middle of another city to explain something to you.

Andrew Michael Roberts and I met in a grocery store in Portland, of all places. I was on my way somewhere and he was on the clock. We haven't met again in this life yet but the words I read in his book the next day haunted me down the street, across the country, through my door and up the stairs. As he wrote in another poem, "god touches you and you are it."[11]

Notes

1. Duncan, 45.
2. Duncan, 45.
3. Levin, 11.
4. Back, 57.
5. Back, 56.
6. Dickman, 36.
7. Dickman, 49.
8. Alexander, 105.
9. Alexander, 83.
10. Roberts, 11.
11. Roberts, 36.

Careless Supplicant

An Interview with Nima Najafi-Kianfar

NIMA NAJAFI-KIANFAR: Kazim, when you're writing, do you think of Islam as a place or a setting? Or do you use Islam as a representation for something else?

KAZIM ALI: Actually writing towards or about Islam has never been a conscious move in my writing. It's taken me a long time to see the connections I have made between things we are given in Islam and how those things affect me spiritually. For example, during Prophet Mohammad's night-journey to Heaven he was given many new instructions; one of the most important was the changing of the qibla or direction of prayer from the Far Mosque in Jerusalem to the Near Mosque, the Kaaba in Mecca. So on the one hand you are supposed to worship what's close to you and not what's far away. But why exactly is the Kaaba holy? Is it because it was built by Abraham on the site of Hagar's exile? The house itself is empty inside and no one is allowed to enter except once a year someone goes in to sweep the interior. So at the center of worship is emptiness? But on the other hand, when the Prophet got on the winged horse that was supposed to bear him to Heaven it launched in the air and first landed on the rock in Jerusalem and then launched itself from there into Heaven. So though you maybe are supposed to worship the near thing, it's the thing that is far away that is the actual route to Heaven. Too, there has been historical disagreement about the actual location of the so-called Far Mosque. Rumi dispensed with the controversy by declaring "The farthest mosque is the one within you." If you take this in light of the statements above it comes very close to the Vedanta and yoga philosophies of the Hindu Vedas. So where does that leave you? Wrote Iranian poet Sohreb Sepehri, "I am a Muslim/ the rose is my qibla,/ . . . / Like a light breeze, my Ka'aba drifts . . ." (Sepehri, 13).

NNK: In your essay "The Architecture of Loneliness" you incorporate and draw from Cristina Peri Rossi's book *State of Exile* and you mention that, perhaps, the poems themselves were her "key to the house in Toledo," referencing, in a way, the Jewish Diaspora. Can poetry be our home? Can poetry be our homeland?

KA: One wants to say that language is the only homeland. We do carry it into exile along with clothes, customs, food. Communities in exile tend to hold on desperately to what existed at the moment of separation. The version of Spanish spoken by Ladino communities (Spanish Jews exiled in the fifteenth century) bears much more relationship to the Spanish of that age than to modern Spanish. I think the Palestinian poet Mahmoud Darwish, about whom I also wrote in that essay, has done more than any other writer to bring the condition, punishments, and prizes of exile into poetry, both in terms of its form and language. And ironically, people who fled their houses in Jaffa and Haifa to escape the war took their keys and only what they could carry, intending to return after the war. They were not permitted to return and their houses are now lived in by others, their furniture, their clothes, their objects of art are all belongings of other people. What appeals to me immensely about Peri Rossi's book is that it is so purely personal and not sociological at all. She writes in a couple of places about larger themes, but mostly it is about coffee, a dog in the street, things her mother used to warn her about . . .

NNK: Okay, let's take that purely personal—the coffee, a dog, and the things her mother used to warn her about—and connect it to the Far Mosque with Sohreb Sepehri in mind. Is the ultimate journey, as is reminiscent of Rumi, the one we take within ourselves—is the ultimate destination simply inside of us? For instance, how do you challenge what is around you in order to reach and discover what is within you?

KA: Well, I think what's inside and what's outside are the same material. Certainly the same physical and spiritual struggles as they relate to the external environment of the planet exist in relation to the internal environment of the body. We're each as individual bodies governed by the various "bodies" of external control—the corporation (body of capital), the government (body politic), organized religion. I think what Sepehri was getting at was that there is a purely internal and individual experience with the transcendent (whether money, god, or

18

power, all of which transcend the individual human body and its small concerns) that is untouchable and unquantifiable.

NNK: In "The Architecture of Loneliness," the self constructs our loneliness. You write, after looking at Mahmoud Darwish's "A Poetry Stanza/The Southerner's House," about how Darwish wishes to transcend the "alienation and the barriers between objects and people." Later, you add, "nations and even languages are mere fictions." I'm wondering: can people transcend that alienation especially when everything around us is fiction?

KA: We have been given this life to try. But let me say something else about it. Darwish's memoir *Memory for Forgetfulness* tells the story of the first day of Israeli bombing of Beirut in August 1982. Darwish is woken in the early morning by bombs and it becomes clear that the tall apartment building on whose 3rd floor he is living has been struck by a missile on the higher floors. Darwish walks on his hands and knees down the long hallway from his bedroom to the kitchen, reasoning that if he is to die he will die not as an animal but as a human—meaning he is going to make himself a cup of coffee in the Arabic style before he ventures to leave the apartment. Because of the poetic nature of the memoir you are left to wonder what he is creating this as a metaphor or whether this was a real event in his life. In my mind I tend to think the latter.

NNK: In your book *The Fortieth Day*, there is a poem that I am drawn to that is titled "The Art of Breathing." This poem deals with that transcendence from the alienation that separates us from ourselves as well as our world, but it also unites us by giving us a scene from the Bhagavad Gita where Arjuna debates whether or not to attack Karna, his cousin and kin. First, what made you decide upon the Bhagavad Gita in your poem/poetry? Second, is there a statement of unity here? Is there a statement of some kind of unity throughout your poetry? And, finally, how can writers destroy their own alienation—as you quote Krishna telling Arjuna that by shooting Karna he will destroy his own alienation?

KA: Well, at least part of that poem's subject is whether one should want to destroy one's own alienation. One's alienation (or anger, or sadness, or selfishness) is part of one, yes? It is a hard, hard choice for Arjun to make and I am not sure I am utterly convinced by Krishna. So perhaps I am condemned to countless more lives in which to work it out, but that too is a form of a gift I suppose.

The poem itself came when I was writing an essay about the poet Reetika Vazirani. She had herself written an essay years earlier called "The Art of Breathing," which was ostensibly about her relationship to yoga (it has been anthologized in a collection of essays about yoga), but which I found to be truly fixated on the fact of her father's suicide. Vazirani, later that summer, also committed suicide and so I found myself in this really vexed position of trying to think about yoga and why it could not save these people from literal self-annihilation, compounded by the fact that a lot of yoga philosophy is about a metaphorical act of "cessation of identification with the mind's fluctuations."

Those "fluctuations of the mind" are what we Westerners commonly think of as the "self," but yoga is trying to teach you that those are not the self at all. In yoga the mind, or sense-making organ, is not the self but only another organ (different from the actual physical tissue of the brain).

The poem came out of all of that thinking and I suppose was a meditation on the possibilities and fears inherent in this destruction of alienation. Because Karna, though the general of the opposing army is not actually Krishna's distant cousin as everyone supposes, but secretly his half-brother. No one discovers this until after the battle is over and Karna has been killed. Alas.

NNK: Coincidentally or intentionally, the poem after "The Art of Breathing" is "The Far Mosque." You state in the notes section of *The Fortieth Day* that this poem is spun around some lines from Rumi's poem of the same name. Is there a connection between Rumi and your book *The Far Mosque*? For this poem, what was the process you employed in order to capture a part of Rumi and maintain your own voice? Was it the subject matter that attracted you originally?

KA: Rumi is in my head conceptually. I only know him through the English translations, most of which have been made from later Turkish translations of Rumi's actual "writing," which wasn't written but recited and copied. I've found lines of Rumi in Vedic writings but I don't know who is quoting whom and I don't think it matters. In my poem "Dear Rumi" I really just had to dream him, trance him, spin him from air. I was not formally or linguistically influenced by most of the translations of Rumi I have read, many of which are done by translators not versed in the original language or familiar with Rumi's historical or cultural contexts. Certainly only a fraction of Rumi's work is currently being translated, and it was not meant primarily as solely literary production but happening within the framework of spiritual discourse.

I became unsatisfied with the end of the poem "Dear Rumi" in which I tried to figure out how Rumi was able to overcome the crippling loss of his teacher and friend Shams-e-Tabriz. I found a spiritual answer in that poem, but the fact of grief is so physical and so much about one's physical position in the world that I needed to revisit the subject matter once again in a poem called "Dear Shams." [now included in *Sky Ward*—KA]

NNK: How important are other poets' poetry for you in the creation and development of your own poetry? Is it a necessity? Should it be a necessity for all aspiring writers?

KA: Absolutely critical for me. Olga Broumas, Jean Valentine, Fanny Howe, Donald Revell, Lucille Clifton, Meena Alexander, Myung Mi Kim, Jane Cooper, Mahmoud Darwish, Agha Shahid Ali, and Susan Howe have all been tremendous, unspeakably important influences in terms of how I try to approach the poetic form. Also in terms of just sheer bravery to speak at all. I also read lots of poetry by my peers and am amazed by the richness and beauty of the contemporary poetry being written. Often I feel something akin to shame that my own writing doesn't take as fierce risks with either language or subject.

I have a wide range of influences though and draw much from visual artists like Makoto Fujimura, Zhao Wou-ki, Agnes Martin, and Hans Hofmann, from dancers Jose Limón and Kazuo Ohno, from musicians and composers like David Lang, Pauline Oliveiros, John Cage, and Yoko Ono, from filmmakers Wong Kar-wai, Maya Deren, and Satyajit Ray. There are so many different writers and artists that feed me. Carole Maso has been a deep and abiding influence on my prose and through her I learned to speak Woolf.

For example with my book of memoir/poetic essays, *Bright Felon: Autobiography and Cities*—I wanted to write a book in bits and pieces. I wanted to talk about my life. The breath and bravery to do it came from reading Meena Alexander's memoir *Fault Lines*, the architecture of it as a book in pieces came from reading Nathalie Stephens' book *Touch to Affliction*, and the microscopic level of how it moved from sentence to sentence and image to image was supported by a reading of Joshua Marie Wilkinson's earlier books. Beckett and Stein lurk there too in the cabinet of influences. You would read this book and perhaps not see any connection at all, but those were the secret sources. Of course Maso's as well as David Markson's works are quite obvious influences in terms of form and style. Many writers are drawing from their privileging of the sentence over the paragraph, including recent prose books by Sarah Manguso, Evan Lavender-Smith, and Michael Joyce, though all three of these use the technique in very different ways indeed.

NNK: I noticed, while reading as well as after having finished *The Fortieth Day*, your continuous incorporation of numbers, seasons, instruments, letters, and various images of water. Were you aware of these thematic elements while working on *The Fortieth Day*? Or did you become aware of them appearing later, after the editing process or, perhaps, after others pointed them out?

KA: Some of these themes developed over the long course of writing the manuscript. But a lot of the recognition came at a later stage. I did not thread them through with intention, though after I started to see patterns I was able to consciously shape. For example I had a single three-part poem that was about a correspondent who would not answer the writer. I later split this poem up into its three parts and scattered them at the beginning ("Vase"), middle ("Interrupted Letter") and ending ("Suture") of the book. I also found myself with a sequence of poems called "Morning Prayer," "Afternoon Prayer," "Evening Prayer," and "Night Prayer," which originally I opened the four sections with. It later seemed to feel better and make more sense for those poems to come second in each of the four sections of the book.

Other patterns emerged not only within the book but between books. There are poems in *The Fortieth Day* that quote lines or images from poems in *The Far Mosque*, for example the poems "Dear Sunset, Dear Avalanche," and "Sleep Door," which each quote lines from the same poem in *The Far Mosque*. This was not intentional but the case of me writing the same line twice. There are hidden (and not-so-hidden) sequences within and between the books as well. *The Far Mosque* ends with a poem called "July," while *The Fortieth Day* includes a poem called "August." The poem "Dear Lantern, Dear Cup" picked up the prominent imagery from the poem "Morning Prayer" and expands on it. So there is a lot that was composed, but only after seeing what was emerging from the surface.

For example in my new book manuscript [now published as *Sky Ward*] it was only after I put the full manuscript together that I found how many drowning boys there were in the book. I'd been writing about the image of drowning since The Far Mosque, but here you had actual boys drowning, building boats, being abandoned in the middle of the ocean. At first I thought they were all different boys—there was Pip from Moby-Dick, there was Icarus, there was Ishmael—but as I revised and looked closer I found them all to be Icarus. There is a sequence now that is threaded through the book, Icarus flying, Icarus falling out of the sky, Icarus floating in open water, Icarus sinking below the surface. The myth ends there—the boy drowns. But in my book the myth continues. Come to think of it, my novel *Quinn's Passage* ends with Quinn in the ocean, beneath the surface of the ocean, trying to decide whether he should breathe or drown.

NNK: Why do you tend to access drowning and the ocean?

KA: I can only guess. Perhaps it is my profound and untouchable loneliness. Maybe because sometimes in the living world I can't breathe. Perhaps rather it is my metaphor for the individual soul adrift in a divine consciousness he does not recognize as such. So in a way it is not a fear of drowning that drives Quinn, but a desire to drown. That's dark. While proofing my new novel *The Disappearance of Seth* I found in it a scene where Seth forcibly holds another character, Adil, underwater. But in the scene it is not played as metaphorically at all; it's a scary moment in fact because Seth thinks he is being playful but Adil is panicked and swallowing water.

NNK: What is your editing process? And should writers consider working with thematic elements when constructing a collection or other literary endeavors?

KA: I cannot write sequences with intention. I think of "subject" of a poem the way I think of "subject" of a painting. Georges Braque said, "I can never plan the painting before beginning, I insist that it make itself under the brush. The painting is not finished until the original idea has been obliterated." I think it is important to work. In my novel *The Disappearance of Seth*, I had six main characters and several very supporting characters. One of those, Jack, kept popping up over and over again. I wrote more and more about him. The people who read the book kept commenting to me about Jack. Finally in the last revision of the book, I saw all the threads come together and wrote several new chapters, and he is one of the main characters of the book now.

I write lots of things at once and then have to work on them all, together, over the course of time. Frequently there is a break for me where I have to put things away and work on new things and then go back to them. *The Far Mosque* I put away in October 2003 and did not look at it again until August 2004. *The Fortieth Day* I started writing in October of 2003 and put away in August of 2004 until about May of 2005. I worked on a third manuscript in the 2005–2006 academic year—this is the book, about forty pages of handwritten poetry (I write by hand until at least the third or fourth draft of a book and then I type into the computer to revise the typescript) that I lost. The rupture of losing that book transformed the manuscript of *The Fortieth Day* because I went back and included poems from memory from those lost pages.

NNK: *The Fortieth Day,* much like "The Architecture of Loneliness," deals with matters of identity and place and the belonging nature of us, as a people, within both of those contexts. Can I assume that identity and place play important roles in your literary developments? For instance, the last line of your poem titled "August" states, "What you seek to fit into will not cease." How important is connection, belonging, and finding yourself/ allowing others to find themselves to you and your work? I know I don't need to point out that your first poem in *The Fortieth Day* is titled "Lostness."

KA: A lot of the drama comes from the fact that an individual wants to join with the larger consciousness (call it Divine if you want, or call it community) but wants to preserve itself, wants to know itself. Can you have both? When I lost my poems I wasn't sure how I was ever going to write again. I was sitting on a meditation cushion trying to meditate, which is the last place in the world I wanted to be, staring at a blank wall in silence, when the first two lines of the poem "Lostness" came into my head. So I went from there to silence. This poem itself has no subject, or I should say the poem interrupts itself and a new subject appears. It does not turn thematically but sonically from the word "rain" to the word "train," and so in that sense the new realization is purely unplanned.

I am lost—aren't all of us? The single narrative poem in the book, "Four O'Clock," which also closes the book, seems to encompass all of these themes into it; it is a completely true story of the time my grandfather went off to buy chocolates and then didn't show up at home when he was supposed to. The police eventually found him wandering around the neighborhood eating those chocolates, lost, and drove him home.

NNK: How much do you depend upon your own life in order to give to the life of poetry? I suppose I am seeing poetry as a living thing; do you believe poetry to be alive?

KA: I am alive. Language that moves through one is likewise alive—though it can do fantastically destructive things. One hopes, in an age when the flow of capital and resources from place to place on the globe has become more important than the flow of blood through the circulatory systems and breath through the respiratory systems of the billions of individual human bodies on the planet, that poetry and art can lead back to ourselves from this alienated and disembodied state we have now found ourselves in. As Regina Spektor touchingly sings, "Suppose I kept on singing love songs/just to break my own fall . . ."

NNK: Yes—exactly—those lyrics actually remind me of a moment in your poem "Horizon" where you deal with the discovery of one's self through the discovery of one's world—as unknowable as it may seem. I see them resonate in your lines, "At its freezing point wind shatters" and "send me to the earth's end—I have never seen it." After it shatters, wind will become wind again, but what can be gained by seeing the earth's end? In "Horizon" I feel a withering inside; you start me off "numb in the storm wanting an answer" and I am left wondering what is the answer? Or what is the question for which we all need/want an answer? The irony here is that at the earth's end I could only find more questions—

KA: Where is the horizon? It's not a real place. It disappears upon approach. It is the limit of sight—nothingness. In Moby-Dick, Pip goes inside because he sees nothing but nothingness and then in his mind sinks below the surface of the sea. Paul Virilio says the horizon used to be the lip of the infinite, but now that limit is the screen. And in the screen is not the nothingness of the horizon but the everythingness; so, we have to contend with a new form of insanity—the insanity of everythingness, the saturation of signs as Baudrillard put it.

How do we get through it? I don't know; I'm still thinking about it.

Doubt and Seeking

A Conversation with Ilya Kaminsky

Note: For this conversation, Ilya sent me a long list of questions in advance. When he was visiting Cleveland, we sat down and spoke at length while he recorded the interview. He later transcribed and edited this conversation, removing the questions and making his role invisible; what remains appears like an essay but it is very much a transcript of a spoken document, one which only actualized through the collaboration of conversation. It has been slightly re-edited for this publication. Actress Katie White's powerful performance in My Name is Rachel Corrie, *the one-woman play based on Rachel Corrie's diary, gave me much insight into Corrie and her motivations.*

In the Islamic tradition, when a baby is born, the father will whisper the calls to prayer (there are two different kinds) into the baby's ears. I feel I've been hearing my father's voice my whole life, in my ears and in my memory. He recited a lot of the Quran when we were younger, and that was my first introduction to poetry. My mother used to sing the Urdu lamentations for Imam Hussain during Muhurram. She also has a beautiful, musical voice. I grew up hearing lots of poetry. Secular poetry is recited, but sacred poetry is always sung or chanted in some way. I remember the music most of all.

I never thought of myself as a spiritual or religious poet, though I've been framed that way. Once my first book came out, and I started doing readings, and interacting with people and talking about poetry, they would say to me, "You're a religious poet." After this was said to me so many times, I decided to consciously explore the topic more, in my second book, *The Fortieth Day*. In *Bright Felon*, rather than being in a mode of unconscious effort, I returned to being aware of this influence or context to my experiences, but tried to see the weave between spirit and material more clearly. But I never planned to be a religious poet. I'm moving in different directions now. Maybe I don't really have anything more to say about it at the moment and need to think more deeply before writing more. Part of my reticence is that I feel very fluid about what I believe. I'm not certain about too many things. Fanny Howe writes that "doubt" and "bewilderment" can be really fruitful, powerful, spiritual places.

Sometimes I think you just have to take a rest, to stop thinking about something for a while. For the moment I might be finished thinking about spiritual things so actively, though maybe it will come up for me again.

I have written about faith because I want to understand it; I want to be included in it. Are we "creatures" or "creations?" There seems to be a difference that etymology can't protect us from. Are we divided shards of one another or are we individuals? What do we owe and what are we owed? They are not just questions of God and the expelled humans, but questions of the individual and the polity. How are we supposed to live together at all (except by empire which means control which can *only* come from force and the threat of the application of violence) unless we can answer these questions?

When I was young, my dad was an engineer on a hydroelectric project to build a dam in the far north of Canada. We lived in a trailer park town, a temporary town. I'm not sure if it still exists, actually. I remember fir trees that were monstrously high. Other than those trees, it was barren. I didn't see leaves turning colors, for example, until I was about 10 years old. I would read stories where kids climbed trees, and I couldn't understand how they did that, because the trees I knew were all so high, with straight trunks like masts of ships, and there were no lower branches.

When the hydroelectric project was done, when I was about ten, we moved to New York City. So I moved from a town of maybe 500 people to Staten Island, which was a shock. We stayed there for only a year and then moved to Buffalo. A couple of years ago when I decided that I wanted to write more autobiographically, one of the things that came out was how much I had moved. I went to college in Albany and stayed there altogether for six years, but after that I lived in a series of places (Washington, DC, New York City, upstate New York), most of these places for only a couple of years. When I started writing *Bright Felon*, it was with the earnest desire to uncover why I was so afraid, why I was so silenced. I wanted to track back through my life, and as I was doing that, I discovered that *place*, specifically moving from one place to another, had such an effect. I barely had any close friends because every couple of years I was picking up and moving, and would have to start over. Of course this partially caused my feelings of alienation and silence, but partially it was because of those same feelings. As Anaïs Nin wrote, we are constructed not linearly but in spirals of energy, always tracking backwards.

I've always been on my own, a single person in the field of physical matter, on his back looking up into oblivion. You can search alongside others, but I don't think others can help you understand your own nature, or if they can it is much further along a spiritual journey than I am. There have been times when teachers appeared to me, but it was always a single person, a single person I had to be smart enough to follow and not always a wise old man with a beard (though it was once!—dear Jonji Provenzano, construction worker by day, yoga instructor by night). They have been teachers of various sorts, sometimes children, sometimes people who were trying to hurt me, figures of substance appearing, trying to get me to look at myself, to see something. But to join with others in a gesture of similitude—I can't draw anything from that, or at least at the moment have not been able to. I'd rather be wandering in a trance through the streets of a busy city, peeling an orange and whispering to the universe than sitting in a pew listening to a sermon or kneeling on a rug reciting chapters.

I fast during Ramadan every year. For me, fasting is a visceral experience: it uses the body to sharpen or affect the mind. You could argue that prayer is the same in its ritual forms, but prayer means less for me, though the early morning prayers which you pray alone, and the afternoon prayers which you pray silently, mean more to me than the evening prayers which are usually prayed with the whole household. I guess I am a loner, or lonely, or the only sum of something. I don't rule out a future in which I do perform these prayers or perhaps am not fasting anymore. Like the fasting month, which with the moon travels backward through the solar year, our spiritual lives shiver and change, like flames, throughout the linear shape of our body's fleshly life in time.

I don't live close to my parents and do not see them as often as I would like. But during Ramadan, when I am up in the early morning hours getting food, I know my mom is awake somewhere, too. There's a closeness that is still there no matter how much time or distance has come between us. Fasting is a practice of restraint and a practice of *action,* both at once. It's the most impossible thing I have ever done and also the most fruitful and intense in experience.

I started writing poems about spirituality and religion as a way to grasp what I believed and try to think things through. Now I've written an entire book about spiritual practice [*Fasting for Ramadan*]. It's about fasting, and it is the culmination of my thinking about religious matters. So it might be time for me to keep quiet about this for a while. If you talk all the time about something, you stop knowing anything about it. That's the danger in poetry as well. Teaching poetry, I always want to stay fresh. I don't want to have too many certainties about what I think or even how someone should learn poetry.

Because I grew up hearing the Quran and the Arabic prayers, and Urdu poetry and Arabic poetry of mourning, poetry was rhythm and music for me before anything else. The poetry I love the most now is that which traffics in music first before any poetics or sensibility. It's why I adore the most diverse range of poets—Lucille Clifton, Susan Howe, Olga Broumas, Gertrude Stein, Jean Valentine, Gillian Conoley, Agha Shahid Ali.

Often I don't even know what a poem means, and I just love the sound of it, the shape of it on the page. I was reading a poem by Laurie Scheck (from *Black Series)* and going on and on about it to a group of friends. Someone asked me to explain it, and I drew a blank. I hadn't the faintest clue what the poem was about. When I went back and re-read it, I found that far from being opaque and mysterious it had the clearest narrative arc about mannequins in a store window. I just hadn't noticed anything about the actual subject of the poem, I was so wrapped up in the words.

There are moments of real awareness or knowledge that come not necessarily from statement but from the shape of a poem as a whole, from the poem as an experience. Fanny Howe is a poet who has repeatedly done the most brilliant work. And quiet! Quiet, not declarative, not definitive, but subtle, whispering. In her new book, *The Lyrics*, there's a sequence titled "School Daze." It's a wonderful, quiet little poem. It just arrives, shows up and does its thing, and then it leaves. Work like that is what I really hold onto and love.

I grew up in a religious household and had strong beliefs, but I chafed against the restrictions and traditions, and had a hard time figuring out how these beliefs could fit into modern life and life in the West. My parents grew up in India in the '40s and '50s, and came here as adults. They were able to integrate very well. They are happy, well-adjusted people. But for me, growing up in the United States in the '70s, it was a completely different world. I have struggled with wondering do you turn your back on a liberal out-looking secular life in America, and become very conservative or religious? Or do you completely abandon your spiritual practice, and give up trying to integrate the two things? I have cousins who have chosen the first route. If you turn your back on one side or the other, it's easier. It's harder to try to integrate, to bring your cultural and religious upbringing into terms with your daily life as you live it here. My struggle has been to unpack my own identity from the layers of not just the cultural and religious tradition my parents gave me, but the cultural and supposedly secular traditions that are instilled in me by Money, the god of America; like every other constructed god, Money is a jealous god and demands you worship it alone—by getting it, spending it, and getting more of it.

If I'm a Muslim, I'm a Muslim in a number of different ways. Spiritually, what I think about God is pretty much in line with the Quranic idea. This asserts the unity of all creation and the absolute lack of distance between the individual and the divine. God isn't up in Heaven looking down. This is close to what I think.

When I read the stories, such as Adam and Eve, and Joseph in Egypt, and Sodom and Gomorrah, and Moses and the Israelites, that appear in the Quran and the Bible, it's the Quranic stories that really make sense to me. But if you put me in a room with twenty Muslims, we probably wouldn't agree on much. Though if you put any twenty Muslims in a room together, they wouldn't agree on much. Our pluralism is one of Islam's hallmarks. We've never agreed.

One of the tragedies of the so-called fundamental Islam is the attempt to flatten out these differences. The Muslim philosophical tradition, like the Jewish philosophical tradition, has always privileged disagreement and difference, with the idea that the individual seeker has to find his way through. Like Judaism, we don't have an ordained priesthood. We have scholars, and it's the people who are the most learned who become so-called spiritual leaders, but there's no ordination. There's no sacred distinction between the scholars and the people around them. That's very important and interesting to me. In Shi'a Islam, in which I was raised, you select the teaching lineage you're going to subscribe to. My dad follows one lineage and his older brother follows a different teaching lineage. I haven't done this because I can't make such a commitment. I can't turn over my restless mind to someone else. I have had a hard time finding teachers and surrendering my own ego to receive their teaching. It seems like this loneliness is a part of my journey, for this present moment at least.

The histories of the Christian and Muslim and Jewish faith are so connected by history and by theological view. You have mosques that are also temples. The Hagia Sophia in Istanbul is a mosque that is also a church, and is not either of those things anymore. The Mezquita in Cordoba is a cathedral which used to be a mosque. In Spain it's the other way around, because the Christian people won the war. In Seville the huge cathedral is built on top of where the mosque used to be. The courtyard of the old mosque with the Moorish waterways cut through it and the minaret are still there, but the bell tower is built right on top of the minaret. All the way up, you see Muslim architecture, and then suddenly there's a Gothic cap with bells inside. The melding of the architecture reflects the ways that the religious traditions themselves are connected. Christianity had its reformation and moved further away, but the deeper you look into Jewish faith and traditions and practices, and Islam, the more you see that it's very much the same religion. If you look at Orthodox Christianity, you can see more confluences there.

I suppose there's a connection between the multiplicity I find in the Abrahamic religious traditions and my writing. Everything can be two things or three things, and I often find myself doubled back in my writing, writing lines in a poem that can switch meanings by the end, or writing a second poem that goes against the meaning of the first one, or writing a poem that answers an earlier one. I'm drawn to the idea of plural thought and multiplicity, like the convex mirror in the Mogul ceiling, which Agha Shahid Ali wrote a poem about. There are reflections in all different directions. You can see two things at once, but both things can be true.

There's a story that the Muslim invaders burned down the Library of Alexandria, but it's not true. The library was actually destroyed by one of the Christian Bishops who ordered all the Pagan knowledge destroyed. In modern times, with some of the splinter movements, we've seen actual actions like this historical one that had been misattributed to Muslims—the Taliban defacing the Buddha statues, for instance. But a disrespect of other religious traditions is not something historically that has happened in Islam. In fact, it's been precisely the opposite. There's always been respect of other traditions. Historians of Jewish history acknowledge the period of the golden age of Jewish civilization as existing in the western Islamic kingdom of al-Andalus, where there was religious tolerance, and Jewish counselors served in some of the highest levels of the government of the Caliph. This new tradition of Muslim and Jewish people being in opposition to each other is a strategic fabrication that started with the Christian powers in Medieval Europe and continues into the modern age, when they still manage to get these people battling each other.

Peacemaking is dangerous when powerful men and their god, Money, want the war to continue. I think of the bodies of Rachel

Corrie and Layla Al-Attar, two women who lost their lives in the Middle East, ten years apart, but each putting her body on the line for peace and peace-making. Rachel Corrie was attempting an American kind of civil disobedience by standing in front of an Israeli bulldozer that was trying to destroy some Palestinian houses. The driver claims not to have seen her, but no one really believes that. And if you have the stomach to watch the video of her death you will see very clearly what the truth is. Layla Al-Attar, on the other hand, was not an activist in the formal sense. She was a painter and director of the Saddam Arts Center, the national gallery of art in Baghdad. She spent her life creating art, strange and lovely paintings, many of which were destroyed when one of Bill Clinton's "precision" missiles accidentally hit her house while aiming for a military target. Her death, in Iraq in 1993, is widely considered to have been purposeful because she had been a vocal critic of the United States and regularly spoke out against the embargo of Iraq and continued air raids over Baghdad as being against international law. As an artist of some stature, her words had impact both within and outside the country, since she had just recently represented Iraq at the Venice Biennale. Her death is one of the most sordid and shameful episodes of the long shameful episode that is America's covert and overt involvement in the politics of Middle Eastern nations.

What can a poet do? What can a writer do? What can a citizen do? The answers to these questions are not separate. Rachel Corrie's actions (you know this by reading her published journals) progressed not out of single intellectual moments of discovery but from her entire life of karma and behavior. She couldn't have done other than what she did, which is to stand up for those people on that day in the extreme and dangerous way that she chose. You can hear in her diaries her desperation swelling day by day until her final actions seem inevitable. The bulldozer was not the rock on which Rachel Corrie broke, but rather she broke that bulldozer. It is the body of Layla Al-Attar, struck in the earliest morning hours, that destroyed the missile we sent, destroyed every other missile in the world.

As a gay person and a Muslim, as both of those things at once, as someone who questioned established political, social, and gender norms, I had a long, long way to go before I could ever speak myself. It is easy to fetishize or romanticize silence when you *are silenced*. I was silenced by myself in this case, but silenced nonetheless. Though in understanding God or death—two of the things we humans really want to know about—you have to come to terms with silence in one way or another. Some poets want to talk into the silence, sound out its limits, and others want to explore that edge of silence, what happens to the world when you look out at it from the lip of the unknown. Some poets do both of these things. I think I am in the third category, though I have traveled there from the second: I could never go into the cave of metaphorical silence, not until I had *learned* myself how to speak. I love that verb "learn"—in Urdu it means both "learn" and "teach."

I think we have a long way to go in America toward understanding and respecting "difference" of all kinds, and toward changing our own behaviors (personal but also national) that stem from a lack of understanding or willful misunderstanding of difference. Sometimes it seems the "American Way" is to want everyone to love money and not have any problems with oppression or colonialism; if you're against the war in Iraq or if you're against the war in Afghanistan or if you're against the global pancapitalist structure that not only allows your superfluous overspending but *actually requires it* for sustenance, then you are practically unpatriotic. American military spending has always been strategic, and it's always been about promoting American power abroad. If you're against that, then you're against the idea of the nation of America somehow, and you're a traitor. Being Muslim, it's if you don't do this, this, and this, then you're not Muslim, and you're not a part of us, and we exclude you. It's all the same kind of destructive thinking. It's not about the human; it's not about the individual spirit.

But I feel that I've found my community in different places, among people who accept me in all of my confusions and misapprehensions—misspellings, errata, like the errata in a book. As humans we just don't make very much sense. Other poets, other religious people, other confused people, other crackpots, rebels, outsiders, these are the people who seem to be my community.

Prayer is speaking to someone you know is not going to be able to speak back, so you're allowed to be the most honest that you can be. Prayer is when you're allowed to be as purely selfish as you like. You can ask for something completely irrational. I have written that prayer is a form of panic, because in prayer you don't really think you're going to be answered. You'll either get what you want or you won't. It feels to me like a sort of panic, a situation where you're under the most duress. Often people who are not religious at all, when suddenly something terrible happens, they know they have to pray. I don't think there's anything wrong with that. We all engage with the spiritual at different counterpoints. Prayer is not a refuge or shelter, so much as it is an opening of arms, an acceptance of whatever storms exist in the world. You don't really pray for your situation to change, you pray to be able to handle your situation. It's not the world you want to change, it's you that you want to change.

My father and I took a trip to Cairo together, which I wrote about in an essay called "Faith and Silence." We visited the Sayeda Zainab shrine and the mosque down the road, where Sayeda Zainab, the granddaughter of Prophet Muhammad, brought the remains of her decapitated brother to be buried. These are places of pilgrimage for Muslims. I felt confusion about the different stories, whether she had really come to Cairo and not died in Damascus, as some believe, and whether her brother's remains are really there. For my dad, the question of what actually happened in this place was less interesting. He knew that it was a holy place because thousands of people were there praying. His view was that regardless of what happened there, it's become a holy place, because it's a repository for all these prayers. People have come there and have made it holy.

If our prayers can make a place holy, then it must mean that there's some divine energy that moves through a human body. In the ancient thinking, that divine energy is the breath of the body. The word in Arabic is *ruh*, which means both breath and spirit. In Latin, *spiritus, spiro* is for spirit and breath both.

As for pilgrimage to holy places, I *do* believe in the spiritual energy that we ourselves imbue places with, and think intense actions can make a place holy. I went to Laramie, Wyoming, last year and I begged my hosts to take me (likely through feet of snow and onto private property) to the place Matthew Shepard waited through the night to be saved. I felt that even though the fence is gone, torn down by the property owners, you couldn't change what happened there, the awful witnessing of everything human. Nearly everyone I talked to about it was really ambivalent (for various reasons).

So I wonder about what Sohrab Sepehri wrote, "I am a Muslim: the rose is my *qiblah*, the stream is my prayer-rug."

For Sepehri, every place in the world was imbued with this spiritual energy and to *choose* a locus for that essence, whether a mosque or church or lonely fence or fenceless field, was to miss the energy completely, the real energy, the feeling in air around your body in every minute. Later on in this poem, he says "My Ka'aba drifts on the wind from orchard to orchard and town to town." What a wonderful loosening of divine from fixed place— there could be no more fixed place than the Ka'aba—to a sort of drifting attention over the landscape of the countryside . . .

Disappearances

An Interview with Britney Gulbrandsen

BRITNEY GULBRANDSEN: I love that you infuse poetry into your novel, *The Disappearance of Seth*, for example, the lines, "The streets are coiled serpents. / A human spine can root the earth to the sky. / The line of white exhaust that writes the sky." Will you explain how this happens?

KAZIM ALI: I was really following the chaotic mentality that followed the days after September 11. I think we were (maybe still are?) crazy that we so quickly left behind empathy and attempts at understanding the world around us in our insane bloodlust and mania for more killing, more bombs, more death, endless, endless war. My characters were like the little bits of paper and ash that were blowing through the city in those days.

Of course the narrative shifted backward and forward because how can you understand anything about history, anything at all about cause and effect when you live in a world on fire, a world governed purely by financial interests and institutions (the Bush White House) whose only purpose is to protect, promote and expand those interests? I didn't need WikiLeaks to tell me half the things it told me—I knew all that stuff and so did anyone else who was paying attention.

So the language of poetry, those lyric interruptions, the places language couldn't bear itself, they became the only way to tell the actual truth, which in this case, as has always been the case, was lies. I had these seven characters, Saif and Salman, cousins, Adil who is their nephew, Zel and Layla, who are Saif's friends but also know Salman, there's Seth (of the title) who is a young man who works at Zel's restaurant, and finally Jack, who knew Seth in high school but is also Salman's ex-boyfriend.

Each of them has a narrative voice and a perspective that moves from the present into the past and all seven of these characters intersect with each other in expected and unexpected ways.

Oracles began speaking in tongues to address what was literally "unspeakable" truth. And only in fiction could I find a golden thread out of the labyrinth of war-mad revenge. Only in this chorus of voices could I find the story I wanted to tell.

BG: In *The Disappearance of Seth* you write, "How can you preserve awareness of a single moment in time?" Please discuss how this statement relates to your writing and this novel as a whole.

KA: Well, my interest in the book (at least part of my interest) was this thinking about history—how it gets created, what forces it exerts on us. Every moment—Seth walking down a dark street in Brooklyn—has the million other moments leaning on us, affecting us. So you can't really be one place at one time. One of my favorite parts about this novel is that people keep bumping into each other, meeting each other in the oddest places. Seth connects all of the characters physically through his body—he touches each of them, in intimacy, in violence, in need of protection or to protect. Of all characters, only Saif and Seth never meet, never exchange dialog—but they *are* in the same place at the same time once in the novel. That sense of interconnectedness even without one's own knowledge of the connection was such a huge part of my life in New York. So the novel is an evocation of place as well as time.

Once when I was talking to a friend about how I could get the characters of Zel and Layla together she said I should have them meet at the Laundromat, which is a typical place to meet new people in New York. There's no Laundromat scene in the book nor does anyone meet while fighting over a cab, but people meet in bars, on the street, in restaurants, museums, airplanes, youth hostels, bridges, all kinds of lovely places.

There is a scene toward the end of the novel where Jack and Layla, two characters who had never met throughout the entire novel, finally meet. I had been working on the book for years by that point and everything was done, but the ending sort of hovered a little bit, I couldn't figure it out. Finally these two characters, both more of supporting characters throughout the book, came face to face and said a few things to each other. And in that moment the whole book started to sing. How can you explain how this happens?

BG: The format of *The Disappearance of Seth* is so unique. I love the back and forth motion through time, from character to character. How do you choose the right format for your work?

KA: Of course if you are a Woolf reader you would know that I had been reading *Mrs. Dalloway* and also *The Waves* while I was writing this book. I was interested in how subjectivity reaches from one mind to another. In one place in *Mrs. Dalloway* Clarissa has a thought in her internal monologue which Peter is thinking at the same time. It's the smallest thing, but Woolf was riding some kind of psychic wave. Earlier in the book the characters scattered across the city are looking up at the sky watching a plane skywrite a phrase, and then later, as Hugh and Richard leave Lady Bruton's luncheon, she feels connected to them by strings as they walk out of her house and out into the city.

So my characters, the seven of them, sort of represent how we are all connected backward and forward throughout space and time. Saif and Layla are friends in the present moment but later in the novel it is revealed that they must have met through Saif's cousin Salman who met Layla ten years earlier and shared a very intense moment with her. Jack is connected to both Seth and to Salman but Salman and Saif don't come face to face until near the very end of the book. There's a moment when Seth reaches out and touches Salman on the chest. Seth physically touches every one of the main characters and this touch manifests his emotional struggle—whether he touches people in intimacy or in violence. He is touched *by* only one character, Layla. He never touches Saif but he brushes his fingers across a painting that Saif has been looking at. Some forms of contact only *seem* ephemeral.

The original draft of the book was even more fragmented and had no section or chapter breaks or even divisions between characters—it was one long interrupted text. I became interested in that Nostradamus couplet that was floating around after September 11 and how the second line and the first line were apparently written decades apart from each other.

Like this, some characters' effects upon each other are obvious and others very subterranean. I added Jack only in my second draft and to a single scene, the one where Seth first moves to the city. Then he just kept insisting on himself.

BG: You do a beautiful job of evoking the mise-en-scène of

September 11 and its aftermath. What drove you to such an intensely emotional setting?

KA: I needed to keep my eyes and my ears and my mouth open. I learned how to write fiction from Virginia Woolf. And Anaïs Nin. And Carole Maso. And Fanny Howe. And Leslie Scalapino. These writers all choose emotional veracity at the expense of physical description or "realism."

What I wanted to describe was not the bricks and stone of the city, its glass and greenery, but rather the currents of the mind, the map of physical human desire. Layla dreamed of fire, so there was fire always around her. The morning after Seth was beaten nearly to death he woke and heard a sound and didn't know what it was—a bird's wing against the window? He wondered about it for pages.

Zel watched the planes hit the towers from the roof of her apartment building on 8th Street, but you never actually know what she has seen, what she is looking at. The *scene* is not described. You only see how she sees it, how she feels.

BG: In the poem "Interrupted Letter" you write, "the floor above creaking with the weight of / someone who wears shoes even at home." Can you explain this image?

KA: Well, I am South Asian and we don't wear our shoes in the house. They are all lined up at the door or in the closet. So for me the ultimate feeling of alienation, of not knowing where you lived, was wearing shoes at home. So there was no place you could feel comfortable, you see. But for every image that's like that, that comes from bare autobiographical actuality, there's another that the ghost of an amber flicker drew in wind on my skin.

BG: You mentioned that Björk's song "Venus as a Boy" inspired your poem "Persephone as a Boy." I personally feel that other art forms greatly inspire my writing. What role does music—and other art—play in your writing?

KA: I have just finished a long series of poems inspired by the sound and the life of Alice Coltrane ["Ocean Street," published in *Sky Ward*]. She was always reaching toward the unknown and undoing of matter into pure energy. She used voice, breath and strings (she was a harpist) to sing into the cloud of unknowing. She could see its edges and the limits of her own breath by so doing. The connection between voice and art for me is ultimate. The body expresses itself in human terms and we have to learn to pay attention. My yoga practice and studies in dance led me through *The Far Mosque*. After I started to chant and breathe I wrote *The Fortieth Day*. The paintings of Makoto Fujimura led me to my series of poems called "Hours."

So you are led and you are fed. Someone said a bird does not sing to fill the world but because it is filled, but I am rather like an empty thing, filling and emptying and refilling. All matter and energy is dynamic and in a constant state of motion. Open up and breathe in, yes, but then you have to exhale and empty yourself. What then fills that space?

BG: In *The Disappearance of Seth*, you write, "Salman reminds himself, after Karbala, after the towers fell down, after any burning, there's this part too, the embers getting faint, settling themselves into thick drifts of ash, settling themselves into warm sleep." This is so powerful. Explain the impact you wished this statement to invoke.

KA: What Salman is thinking about is that there is an inhale and an exhale, but even those embers fallen have potential to reignite and burn the house down. Rage sleeping inside is still rage ready to burst into flame and destroy everything.

But Salman is someone who is afraid, trapped in his life, unable to really communicate with the people around him. What he is unable to say to his cousin who is his best friend and who grew up with him he is able to say to a complete stranger who he has just met. Saif gets a little bit of a bad rap I think for being cold and intolerant of Salman, but I understand a little bit—Salman has held him at arm's length their whole lives, falsifying a kind of closeness—of *course* Saif would pull away and stop caring.

But it meant a lot to me to write the early scene when they are both thirteen-year old boys, the scene with the sacrifice of the goat. To see how consumed by *jealousy* Salman is, jealousy of his cousin who *isn't* conflicted, who is straight, who is comfortable in his skin, who doesn't have to keep all these secrets—

I revisited that scene in an autobiographical comic illustrated by Craig Thompson, called "Flowering."[1]

BG: I love your poem "Quiz." It was captivating. Where do you get your inspiration for such unique poems?

KA: "Quiz" began when I was teaching a seminar on aesthetic movements of the twentieth century to students at the Culinary

Institute of America. I loved doing it because these were not all students who had backgrounds in poetry and art but they were all very hungry (excuse the pun) to learn. So I was able to introduce them to people like Malevich, Anaïs Nin, Ginsberg, Yoko Ono, Alice Coltrane, Agnes Martin, Virginia Woolf, Mina Loy and many others.

At the end of one of the units I gave them a quiz. It was a matching quiz where you had to match column A and column B. They had to answer it. I revised the quiz after their answers.

I don't think of myself as particularly formally innovative, though experimental approaches help me to transcend the limitations of the small self and access what is beyond intellect and intention.

BG: The titles of your poems are unique, and they do a lot of work. Could you describe your process for titling poems?

KA: It's the hardest thing in the world to do and usually the title comes at the very end after a lot of other work has happened. A title is a frame or an arrow that points you somewhere, so it means something if it is vague or obvious or cryptic, there are a lot of different choices to make. But no, I haven't the slightest notion how to do it. Or how to write poems, thank god.

BG: In *The Disappearance of Seth* you write, "The body remembers what people forget." Explain how this statement relates to your writing.

KA: Because we *do* hold wounds and old hurts in our bodies themselves. My ankle which I sprained badly once is still stiff sometimes, though twenty years later. The mind is excellent at walling off and away deep traumatic experiences, but they still live deep, deep inside, not only within the body but in the psyche itself.

But also that the individual remembers pain or loss and passes it along to others in the form of history, even when the social polity as a whole doesn't process information or think about it. We (the United States) annexed, conquered, bought, traded and/or outright stole every square inch of the continent we are standing on. The vast majority of the treaties we made with the people whose land it was were either abrogated, forgotten or are still in legal contention in the U.S. court system. But is this newsworthy? Do we hear about it on a daily basis? Hardly.

History moves darkly and we are small, soft things. With little voices, perhaps, but voices nonetheless.

Note

1. Published in the Comic Book Legal Defense Fund, *Liberty Annual 2011*, Legendary Comics.

Third Eye Who Sees

On the Source of Spiritual Search in Sappho's
Gymnasium *by T Begley and Olga Broumas*

No matter how much religion is organized, the very wild act of an
individual human soul married to a physical body attempting to
whisper its breath into the universal mouth of endlessness would
be impossible to buckle down to one form, impossible to write
into little books with approved versions. Instead such utterance
must escape free like the screams of Antigone or Electra in the an-
cient Greek plays; between the human and divine there is a place
where language breaks. Such a place too might be called god.

Olga Broumas and T Begley created *Sappho's Gymnasium* in a
collaborative act. They describe their process in an essay jointly
uttered: "But who speaks? A voice of pluracination, heard par-
tially, as always, gracing one of us with particulars, the other with
the hallucinated breath of verbally unintelligible but musically
incontrovertible dictions. That was one time which recurs. An-
other is certitude of the field it requires us to serve—eros: gra-
cious, philoxenous, augmenting, lubricant, remorseless faith."[1]

Every space between two bodies, I once thought, was a place
of danger. But if there is a danger, it is the danger of losing one's
own self, risking transforming into the other. We want to hold
ourselves close. But in between the bodies of the two women,
or—according to Broumas (email conversation)—words origi-
nating in the mouth of one (Begley) and passing through
the breath and mouth of the other into syntax and structure
(Broumas), a third voice, not "disembodied" but actually "re-
embodied," issues forth.

They open the series of lyrics with a quote from Sappho, the
spirit-muse who rules the roost here, for more reasons than

one: "Tears unbecome the house of poets." The transformation here—a rejection of grief or stasis, an embrace therefore of *ex stasis* or "ecstasy"—poetry, really—is by negation or "unbecoming." Unbecoming means to stay in a newborn state or to travel backward even earlier, to whatever that formless state might be. To be "ecstatic" is to be outside of one's own "self"—however that self be constructed.

What house would a poet live in? The gymnasium where one is "nude, trained, exposed" is a school here of language, of joy and poetry. The body utters and the intellect, the part that wants to organize these prayers into sense, is left behind or at least suspends itself for a moment.

"Any utterance runs the risk of being ideological," Roland Barthes wrote, as invoked later in the "Proem" that opens the book.[2] Here the poets, always plural, want to reject the "thought police" and "recorded grammar" and move out on their own, see what can be discovered while—here two make one—lost in the woods of language. The "proem" ends with a series of quotes from W. S. Merwin, ending with this meditation on unity between two bodies making a single work: "Each of us is one/side of the rain/we have only one shadow."[3]

The book is comprised of ten long sequences, each made of small fragments and fractures of poetry that assemble themselves loosely around themes or images. The boundaries between the sections quiver a little bit—when *Sappho's Gymnasium* (excluding the first and longest sequence, "Prayerfields,") was republished in Broumas' collected poems *Rave*, the most significant and obvious difference was the compression of page space that republication can require. Gone were the wide open spaces of the page in which single lines or stanzas would float—the poems instead ran straight in a series after the title. But the more significant difference was that often poems at the end of a sequence would be removed and appear instead as the beginning poems of the following sequence. Some pieces were inverted and some few were excluded. More on this presence of two differing versions of the text later.

"Prayerfields," the longest and opening sequence of the book, is a seemingly autobiographical series of short poems that travel from a position of "invocation" to the lip of "ecstasy." "Invocation" means you are calling on a force outside yourself—a "prayer," not always "for" something, but often that is indeed the case. The "field" of the title also means you are not whole and complete unto yourself, but need to depend on some particular external "location" to create that spiritual matrix in which a communion or communication with the divine or god-like can occur. When you move to the "lip" of ecstasy—the state in which you can travel outside your fleshly confine or perhaps realize the borderless condition of the spirit—it means you are beginning to understand you *are* actually *inside* something, in this case your physical frame and body, inextricably a part of it but also, in fact, Some Other Thing at once.

The form of language cannot contain the impossibility of god. It is one thing to believe in a *via negativa*—that God is fundamentally unknowable—but when you do have to live inside your body and in the actual material world it is not much help. *Via Negativa* means you still believe god can be defined, but in this case defined by what it is *not. Sappho's Gymnasium* does not accept this dichotomy and chooses a third way.

Here is a piece early in "Prayerfields":[4]

best friend and half-wild protector named
comfort for the body I can always
pray keep me in god coherent form
of light like memory also distributed
where it is not dimension only

Each phrase can leak into the other—god as best friend and half-wild protector? Did he (always lowercase in this book) comfort the body? And what is the prayer: to be kept in coherent form or to be kept "in god" and what is coherent—the body or the form of light; these two perhaps can be said to be the same thing—at any rate, body, god and light all wish to be beyond the fact of mere "dimension" or physical shape.

The tender body, the one that is mortal, the one that dies, needs a tender god as well. The human, understanding this walks "out onto the ice finite and helpless in return his soft/ parts ventral know to die." It seems a bitter lesson to learn—that after this glorious awareness, after learning to love one must (we all *must*) learn how to die.

Is that it? We live to love and die? You are on your own but it will have to be enough the poets seem to say in this short pair:[5]

> this helpless desire your own suffering the
> work of grace makes us visible
> flocking on small
> islands of inland waters the near
> shore of unsayable

> each
> had vivid memories of portions of
> their Good Friday experience the only
> one who can initiate you
> is your soul

The usual religious practice of seeking "grace" does nothing more than make humans "visible" on their little islands that hover near what cannot be expressed. It is the drama of "Prayer-fields" to seek to understand not where one body ends and another begins—it was this dilemma that caused Atalanta to lose her wrestling match (and with it her sovereignty) to Meleager—but rather where the human and mortal part ends and the endless spirit matter begins. Is this the border between life and death? Not "life" nor "death" the way we think of it anyhow: solely in terms of the physical body that we can touch and smell and taste and hear and see.

Christ, rather than being the bodily incarnation of God-in-flesh, the key that can open the lock to everlasting life, is instead in this book a "jailer" (22). The "father" to whom one might ordinarily pray or depend on for support is asked to "burn the river down" since once the river, giver of sustenance, disappears one might in the "lighted flexion receive god unspasmed."[6]

The father reappears later:[7]

> father whose voice had not been completely
> destroyed is it okay now
> to love the actual

watchful
young adult genital oral

This is the actual world then that one lives in. The body, even with its spiritual leanings, wants the world genitally, orally, lustfully. Though in a poem that depicts childbirth the poets do say "borderlines they need," between a mother and a child being then created out of the material of her body and through the "movement of her own/body she wishes to be small/again."[8]

"The tablet is broken" could mean here those received laws of the father; though of course those tablets were broken because they were flung by their authority (Moses) at people who were disbelievers.[9] It is as if Creation itself were that rupture, that cells broke apart and multiplied the way those tablets broke.

The body becomes visible through the sunlight of this creation, this rupture. Though Anne Carson has written compellingly about the "erotic" space being the gap between two bodies, here in the gap between the two poets the moment of touch is the transformative moment, not the climax of eros but only the beginning—(or in the space between two women's bodies, lesbian bodies, an argument against the notion of climax?):[10]

if this one holds me so
pleasurable does so long
enough I came visibly to
love

In the closing poems of "Prayerfields" there is a growing awareness of the qualities of the individual body and a recognition that to be able to communicate with "god" or That Name, one does have to use the tools and tricks one has: one's voice, one's bones, the strings in the throat, the so-called box of wonder. Small wonder ancient Indian sages identified the seven places of communion inside the human body, the chakra wheels around which we turn.

only the analyst of souls knows how
to exhume them to the breathing it is necessary
for the caller to anoint
the newborn[11]

We come to language through existence then, or said more directly, through actual breathing. It's the selfsoul here that takes you through, and still one has to be handled, "anointed," or baptized—validated by some external office. Later on in the book the emphasis will move even further out to the intangible, but only once the body is fully understood and "prayer," such as it is, becomes possible at all.

All the speakers want seems summed up in the prefatory one-line "invocation" that opens "Prayerfields":[12]

faithful the present I see you

By the end of the sequence, one doesn't require the locality of the "field," rather, one understands, "the impossible world is/ all around us indistinguishably/one is this act the cause can be/ anywhere."[13]

We attended a birth to understand the necessary way a body separates from another and in this were able to see a microcosm of all creation—cells breaking forth from cells, the entropy of the universe that splits to join, ceases in order to continue. And so later we attend such ceasing:[14]

. . . I sit by the death bed she is
so beautiful a transparence one speaks
is the beginning of
memory of sensation let me make
it good light being unborn

When Sappho suggests that tears "unbecome" a poet, she enjoins a return to initial or original states at the beginning, now one (by "dying") engages not in a ceasing but in a continuance of transformation into new matter and energy: being "unborn." It's not mere euphemism here; it has something real at stake— the poets go on to say "I committed all the necessary murders within myself/to acquire faith." It brings my mind back to Arjuna's argument with Krishna at the beginning of the *Bagavad Gita:* what is it within yourself you are willing to part with in order to transcend the limitations of mind and body both. And what, after all, *is* the "soul"?

Can we at all follow one of the final wishes in the field:[15]

alone daily peace
to honor without coveting
the possibility of life
without meeting boundaries or ever turning back

At the close of this sequence, with this wish to really *know* the body, the boundary between it and the spirit both within and beyond, we are left at another moment of birth: "when this was done an eggshell forms/us light hammering a spasm of sound."[16]

That eggshell may call to mind for the mythologically minded reader Helen herself, born immortal from a swan's egg, pure beauty and brilliant besides (for more on Helen's brilliant mind, see her appearance early in *The Odyssey!*): who better to take us on the next stage of this journey—the drama of the body knowing its own spiritual capabilities, seeing itself not as a limited vessel that prevents spiritual enlightenment but actual vehicle of absolute potential to travel those air-light roads.

From the broad open space of the field to a more concentrated arboreal venue, the opening section of "Helen Groves" sets the stage for the drama to come:[17]

what if there were no sea
to take up the table of our hearts
breath which is everywhere curved
hand from infinity broken (57)

The poets question what the individual will do without the infinity outside and beyond. Now turned inward how could one *not* feel lonely? One does float after all in the saline sea. The "floating" is not merely superficial (one floats by taking enough air into the lungs to remain buoyant—one only sinks, and thus drowns, by taking water into the lungs) but deeper even than that: the result of millions of years of evolution since our emergence from the ocean, the salt content of blood and seawater remains precisely identical. The "heart" then of the sea and the body is the same, a table on which one floats.

What if our anxiety—the anxiety of death, of what will happen to us "after"—is the same as the anxiety of the soul *before* birth: will we be received? What happens on the other side of this existence? Like the question of who we are in a dream this one remains unanswerable. Breath turns in the lungs the way space bends in the universe. A human body is fashioned out of another human body and *somehow* in the womb cells transition from tissue into incarnate being. No one can say when and no one can say really how. Human bodies—flesh—"broken" perhaps from the beginningless store of universal energy that is still to this day being categorized and understood—seen for what it really is: none of it has either appeared nor disappeared, it seems, since the very so-called beginning of time. It has always Been.

So the bodies that broke off, the humans, have a role to play:[18]

Went walking and walking
far off to get water
two people with your birds
mirrors for multiplying light
we serve

Peaceful limbs
had been a little breathless
branches of new humans
the gods are open mouthed

One delight of the queer line breaks and eschewing of any punctuation at all is that sometimes clauses lead both backward and forward. Who are the mirrors meant to multiply light, the birds or the humans? And who is being served?

Humans, at any rate, by dint of the vulnerability of our forms, are tasked with the coarser chores of life. The two humans in this case, peaceful, having walked a long way for water, are breathless. It is unclear whether it is during their breathlessness the gods open their mouths or whether *they* themselves are the gods in question. Either way one is left to consider the qualities of being "open mouthed": exertion, intimacy, communication, desire . . .

"The idea of a book held me as icons hold others," the poets quote Odysseas Elytis in the "Proem" to this book.[19] "I had but to fill it as you fill a row of empty glasses and, immediately, what power, what freedom, what disdain toward bombs and death it gave me." So the book or icon is something to be entered, to be interacted with in some way. Here in "Helen Groves" the poets say, "by long kiss the icon is/worn a lighter color/than the rest of the face/bathing the living."[20]

It is these physical interactions—birth, a kiss, bathing, caressing, sexual intimacy—that bodies come to know each other. The sun-soaked mythology of Broumas and Begley traffics in Greek idiom, landscape and sensibility but runs counter to the myths of alienation so prevalent in the ancient stories: Psyche who should not look, Eros who would not be seen; Orpheus who should not look, Eurydice who could not be seen; Echo who could not speak, Narcissus who would not hear; Atalanta who did not know where bodies ended, Medusa who could not be looked upon, Cassandra who could not be understood, the Sirens who could not be listened to. And so on.

The speaker here, like Homer's Telemachus, is unworried by the question of actual "origin." When Athena disguised as Mentor asks Telemachus whether he is Odysseus' son the young man says with the blithe unconcern of youth, "My mother says I am his son; I know not surely. Who has known his own engendering?"[21] The poets here clarify, "I don't know virgin/when I was made I was made," meaning there's no "blank" state or "pure" state, the answer to that old Zen question of "who were you before your parents were born" seems suddenly to be a somewhat stark though simple "No one." Is it too philosophical for the actual and ongoing world? The body with the mind in it, unaware of the infinity or eternity of the spiritual energy inside, is left with few ways to understanding it:[22]

It's not the herbs on my lips
we have freedom to be
infinite or not at all
infinite or not yet

It's a wonderful little musing, turning away from sensory experiences as a route to spiritual awakening and declaring the right of the human to ignore all this philosophy, to ignore the infinite inside, to be what one chooses to be, though the second choice implies that the awareness is inevitable, one is only left with deciding "infinite" or not yet infinite . . .

Though these poets of course dare to actualize. They confess in the very next poem, "I am optimistic I am scared a little"—how lovely to read both emotions in the same line, unmediated by connective language or comma. "My friend it is possible," they go on to say, "to drink the ecstatic one's ecstasy/over the source of energy I drink it."[23]

"I come single," the poets declare in their twin voice, "alone/ under my clothes."[24] "Alone here" has echoes of what we really *are* under our clothes—naked. In this original state, "alone," profoundly alone, we arrive prepared for the journey. As one reads an echo of "naked" under "alone," one too hears the sexual *double entendre* in the spare declaration "I come."

The supplicant, washed in the eros of knowledge, ready to light the lamp and stare then at its sleeping body, is given a little motivational speech at the end of the section:[25]

> You'll like the worshippers
> the sky with its seacoasts of Greece
> what kind leaves home for home
> send me

Here the seemingly infinite and intangible sky possesses inside itself the physical seacoasts of the former homeland. But there's no nostalgia in it because the poets dream of leaving "home for home," ask then—who is it they are asking?—to be sent. The body then, though explored as an instrument of liberation, is asking here to be acted upon. How can it be? Can you believe in both things at once—that infinity is inside but that the self is still separated from it, that you still must beseech that separate thing, pray *to* it? It seems a contradiction, a return to a more dualistic way of thinking, here in two small words, the first *actual* "prayer" since the initial line of "Prayer Fields."

Prayers in every religious tradition always depend on their being uttered in the "proper" language for complete efficacy, whether—for example—Sanksrit, Arabic, Hindi or Latin. The *intention* of the supplicant is secondary to the breath flowing through and animating the consonants of need.

The word "vowel" from the section "Vowel Imprint" opens with "vow" of course, and opens its mouth to modulate and end on the liquid "l" (a yogic chanter is reminded of pronouncing "Aummmmmm." And the word "imprint" itself "im" "prints" when the close-lipped breath of its first "m" (said by linguists to be a human body's first consonantal pronunciation—in infancy, the mouth surrounding a nipple) meets the "p" (our second sound, the sound the mouth makes upon releasing said nipple).

The imprint of a vowel must be that depression made—on earth, sand or skin—by the breath of another. One also remembers the Islamic version of the story of the Virgin Mary, giving birth under a date palm, alone and ostracized. To give her sustenance the date palms drop fruit into her lap; taking one she expels a breath in pain and the humble date is thus forever imprinted with her breath and made the holiest of fruits.

"Vowel Imprint" contains mostly short utterances or expulsions, some of them only a single line long, as if in effort to pack greater impact into as brief a possible vessel of poetry. Indeed the first line of "Vowel Imprint" is one that has captivated me for years, one which has written itself in breath and in other kinds of ink all along the measures of my skin:[26]

Transitive body this fresco amen I mouth (77)

The vowels of this opening line begin hemmed in by multiple hard consonants of the first word "transitive." They open wider in the word "body," but it isn't until "fresco" with its multiple liquid consonants "f," "r" and "s" that they really open free. The hard "c" of "fresco" causes a little expulsion of the vowel sound. It is notable that the turn from hemming consonants to releasing consonants happens on the neutral word "this." "This" holds a lot of power here—referring to the "fresco," which is of course also the body. The wide open vowels of "amen," "I" and "mouth" open the poem out as breath, though the final word "mouth" of course imitates the body—a vessel container of the boundless open inside—the "ou" in "mouth" is the same as the "Au" in "Aum."

The body is both transitive here, a passage, a bridge of flesh for breath between states of before and after, but also a fresco, made of pieces from all eras of time and all places throughout the universe. If the body is a fresco could it be the eternal matter that is painted onto the flesh of the body? But in a fresco that paint itself has bonded, become part of the wall; they are no longer separable

The appearance of the speaking "I" (relatively late in such a brief poem) is the bridge between internal acknowledgment of infinity—"amen"—and the act of the individual actualizing herself into the external world, the exhalation of breath in "I mouth."

Of course what makes the line *truly* interesting is that it moves beyond standard syntax of prose declaration and into the queer strange language of ecstasy reminiscent of the odd choral ejaculations in ancient Greek drama. It's never fully clear what the subject, main verb, and object of this line are. Is the fresco being mouthed or the body or is the mouth an open space at the end of the line, mere descriptor for the I?

In the short poems of "Vowel Imprint" there is always a challenge or danger in lingering in the half-real zone between the actual physical world and spiritual awareness. At one point the poets worry, "Will these floors burst in oxygen/my life spent swimming."[27] Later they warn, "You feel the bruising mid-flight as one born/to dazzle god with your heat."[28] The encounters between the individual human and her spiritual sound are fraught with the essential difference between asceticism and human needs, the "hot burning off of self which exhausts it."

How is one, as a faulty human, a hungry one, supposed to continue in the face of such dangers? The poets muse:[29]

Honey of clarity and strength laboring light
the yes of song and its relentless ear
the actual words

There's no complicated solution ultimately. The desire toward song, toward affirmation comes accompanied by its "relentless ear." The "actual words" at the end may be song or they may be ordinary human utterance. Or it may be—best of all—that ordinary human utterance *is* song if only we could learn to hear it as such.

Thus reassured the poets realize:[30]

I am not alone
facing the sun
lover of all

Out of all the fragments and lines and scraps of Sappho there is
a single poem to bear witness that Sappho was not mere ancient
postmodern poetess marrying broken phrase with profound in-
sight like Myung Mi Kim or Susan Howe. Her single poem shows
a musical poet working wonderfully within the musical and met-
rical conventions of the time, a poet like Dickinson perhaps. So
among the shreds and shards of *Sappho's Gymnasium,* around
half-way through the book significantly, we come upon the first
page of "Flower Parry," a poem written in a more standard per-
formance mode but with all the metaphysical worries and flur-
ries of the poems that came before and that follow.

This opening poem uses repeated lines almost like a blues
musician repeats lyrics. It's an apt comparison since throughout
Sappho's Gymnasium the poets riff on themes, words and phras-
es:[31]

Clear blue temple I'm taken in
clear blue temple I'm taken in
god would talk if I did
god would talk if I did

got a mouth wants to know

I was seeing someone burst open
I was seeing someone burst open
the door she was being
the door she was being fucked

hurt as a virtue

hurt as a virtue makes me
vertigo piss-scared

seeing someone burst open
god would talk if I did

Is it true then that god demands the submission of the individual ego, so equating spiritual enlightenment with a violence? In which case the idea of being thus "hurt"—that is to say "enlightened"—is not necessarily appealing to the individual person. *Why* should we give up our own individual perceptions, our own distinctive uniqueness? If even under the worst of circumstances we are afraid of change then small wonder we are chary of "realizing" infinity or immortality.

The line that rings in my ear is, of course, "got a mouth wants to know." Who is it that has a mouth? The human "I"? And what is it I want to know? The poem gives no chance to find out. Is it true that god will only talk if we see someone "burst open"? The thought gives scant comfort. Barring actual god-talk or prophecy the poets are left only with their own powers of ecstasy and utterance. As they say in their essay on the collaboration, "I need a wafer, equal in body and propulsion, that develops an entirely immaculate congregation of the tongue so that we might address you in words your love shapes."[32]

"Flower Parry" goes on to challenge the easy notions of obtaining wisdom by exploring some of the real dangers and difficulties that lie in wait for the individual human, the one who has a body and mind vulnerable to attack. "Let go your hammering," one poem begins, saying "I can miss with effort . . . no matter how painful . . . if it came from my heart."[33] In one place the effort of spiritual struggle is not conscious. In talking about a failing garden the speaker observes:[34]

I should rest and not water the
shoots but wait until dark to
uncover them (96)

"God with restraints I'm not," the poets say, as if to re-emphasize that one is caught in a swing between an understanding of "God" in strictly human terms and a refusal to categorize god at all.[35] There seems sometimes in the swinging to be no in-between space. In the closing poem the moment of creation and destruction is explored:[36]

> I don't know why I serve or want to dance wake up be born
> . . .
> I do myself o solitude
> at the birthing of sea level
> my undesired you ask undestroyed

It's the unmentionable things there, the reversed things that exist in the present moment always, actually "unasked" for. In a quest to reach spiritual enlightenment the individual human suffers precisely because the body has its sensory limitations, is trapped in a sensory existence. The lustful supplicant is rife with unquenchable desires so how is it possible to move forward at all? The image of the Fool, first card of the tarot's major arcana, seems suddenly to be the position of knowledge, the simple saint, the sacred idiot, the only one able to achieve wisdom.

The lyrics of "Your Sacred Idiot With Me" splinter into brief and compressed two- and three-line epigrams, almost as if devolving into child speech or baby talk:[37]

> After the roots have spoken
> your night cries

> Look after me true
> true wherever

In these brief moments we are able to grasp or explore insights without some of the verbal and rhythmic fireworks that characterized early sections of the book. The syntax stripped down here, the line breaks less unconventional; yet the extreme compression itself offers a kind of shivering sometimes:[38]

> A soul I did insist upon
> I live superimposed

One thinks of the earlier "fresco" here. If we are superimposed though, superimposed on *what*? What is the nature of the connection itself between the material world and the spirit world? Because if there is a duality between them then spiritual search in the material world must be limited to realm of "preparation;" there will be no achieving in the mortal frame of a life. It might be the job of poetry like this to expose the cracks or rents in our perception of the world and the actual physical world to show the places and possibilities where there is actual transit between the material and spiritual. In other words, "in the visible/time poets shine."[39]

In a hymn or choral ode the language transforms from the plainspoken of the rest of the section into the more ecstatic musically infused rhythms of the earlier sections of the book:[40]

> your translated trance I am performing it
> asylum through my clearest my solid birthright singing
> full time mercy break god

In the first line there is a trance that is given by one person, "translated" from somewhere—from the spiritual realm of formless energy in the of matter, meaning *words*?—and passed along to the other who is then able to "mouth it" or perform it. Here then is the story of the writing/speaking of this book, two poets, Begley and Broumas, who pass the words and lines across the space between them.

The words in this case become an "asylum" or "birthright" both of which imply transitional states—"asylum" meaning a freedom from past oppression or sanctuary with other likeminded individuals otherwise unable to function within mainstream society, and "birthright" which means a reclaiming in some way of something intrinsic which has gone unrecognized or has been lost.

When the poets sing "full time mercy break god," god breaks free in the poem. "He" has been previously mentioned by name very rarely but here god breaks at the end of a line, a chain of associations which evinces not worry or apprehension but rhythmic and spiritual release into open expression.

Wood can be joined to itself by pegs which means held together but by its own material, fastened but not splintered, not pierced. In "Joinery" body and soul, matter and energy or human and human thus weld together and become "structure."

"Long my heart has been/home," one lover may say to another, "home you feel the most/my arms will tell."[41] The limbs of the body narrate the story of lust and love here, as in the Quranic story of the body which speaks of the deeds of the person on the Day of Judgment. If the body can speak out (to divine force in this case, one presumes) then maybe the body can speak inward to the self and not in after-time but now immediately in this-time:[42]

> Art is climax over conduct
> zen of no color by sunrise I do

Perhaps "intention" or motion of the mind into the physical world is what is meant by "art" here, an art which trumps actual conduct. The second line of the couplet uses the language of the vow. Broumas, a Zen Buddhist, has written elsewhere of her work in massage and its counterpoint in meditation practice. She greets this practice of the body without "color," without intention, each and every day. In her essay "Moon," she says, "I have neither hope nor the absence of hope. I have the sweeping."[43]

It seems passive but in the next poem of "Joinery" the poets praise not willingness to sing but the gift of being "willing to be sung."[44] The body itself, the human life becomes expression of something else ineffable, something with agency. Imagine it: that you are not singer but thing *being sung*.

Other metaphors besides joining, music and meditation throughout this section include photography, gardening and sonar location. The actual spiritual symbols aren't all Buddhist though. In one poem the poets consider "reincarnation" with Christian symbols, meant for all supplicants though, not limited here to god (in the form of the Son):[45]

> Cure for water is water
> one very blue throughout the trees

divine indulgence yesterday
the cross dove from the wall
naked cross get into lifeboat
reincarnation of not

It's the "not" at the end of the poem, the doubt that quickly questions everything that came before that really drives the point home: No matter what is believed or disbelieved, no matter what poetry works to reveal, the fundamental unknowability of spiritual conditions is a wall not to be breached. In other words, "My belief and aggression took so long/sowing ground in her prophetic tropic."[46] "I'm done reading your book and admiring you/grape-sized obedience," the poets say tartly in the very next poem. What point is there indulging in this so-called minderror mirror, they wonder.[47]

"There is no way of rainbow for looking is broke/child behind unknown tongue," they say. It is some reassurance to know it is impossible to have any such revelation.[48] After all the looking eye is "broke." Unlike the knowledge that seemed possible at the beginning when the body first broke from infinity, here it seems the eye *can't* see, won't be able to after all. One puts faith then not in the tongue that can speak in the actual world but the other tongue, the unknown tongue.

The path of the artist—and only that one—can lead the human not to revelations that will fill in the blank of received or expected outlines but of the actual confusing world with all of its contradictions, countermandings and, yes, countertexts. "On faith from some artist's image/a sheet of paper saying you are possible," reassure the poets, "values I stand on I invent/and in the very middle of that gap/the givers."[49]

Once more we are left in the space between the seeker and what could be known. Neither can be achieved. Only the material actual physical world can be sensed and perceived by the human incarnate body. What wisdom there can be can only be achieved in quotidian and ordinary things. The body must know its own processes then—birth, love, breath, age and death—to have any hope of deeper connection. Is it possible? That remains to be seen.

"I AM TASTING MYSELF/IN THE MOUTH OF THE SUN,"
June Jordan says in a poem, dreaming herself born of that
(seemingly) eternal source of (seemingly) endless energy.[50]
What's digested by the sun must then be transformed. Birth im-
ages open this section. To contrast the earlier "hand from infin-
ity broken" here we find "spit sharpened so her tongue/finds
the newly torn."[51] The difference between "broken" and "torn"
is that the "torn" does imply an external force acting upon a
previously whole matter, whereas "broken" may be a present
condition which has its own agency, i.e. a small part "broken off"
of a whole but also in itself whole. While it may be a Christian
idea that liberation is dependent on the external factor, whether
"grace" or an actual actor, the Son of God or whoever, there
might also be something to thought that other humans are re-
quired for the liberation of the individual.

"Give me your hand candidate of light," one seeker says to
another, reassuring "the light won't wake you."[52] There is an in-
and-out movement like the tide or breath that enables one to
harmlessly engage with oneself and the community at large:[53]

Language you surge
language you try me
I set a place for you
who would have guessed there were so many
similars to you with your light
plotted across my window
we are walking toward it arm around
shoulder what else

Once again the poem fragments and splinters off at the end
reminding the reader there is more to go, that the journey is
endless process. Besides an ode to language, of course, it is also
an ode to touch, ending with the human connection of one's
arm resting around the shoulder of the other. Language and the
body meet as one here and in many erotic lyrics that thread and
rethread their way through the sequences of the book.

What the poets call the "sunny addiction" and "barely possi-
ble thirst" feels many times like it could equally apply to spiritual
or sexual thirst. "I lie all night with her/I live where she is many,"

the breathless poets intone, "I look forward to it/I get on my knees."[54] As Atalanta thrashes in the moment of being unable to tell whether her body and Meleager's body are actually different, the searcher feels an erotic or ecstatic moment wondering where boundaries of skin truly lie:[55]

> Her hours alone allure
> mind makes mind need to cure
> our work before us shape to be
> receiving skin amid unceasing

If what's "digestible" is something that passes through the Sun, or the energetic power of the universe, the "insomniac" must be someone unable to interface in any meaningful way with the restorative and intangible energies of the universe. Sleep thus denied, the conscious mind moves into a different and skewed relationship with the reality around one. "The light upon me a kind of body," the insomniac realizes suddenly in her sleep-deprived clarity. Talking about the woods, she thinks, "the twigs snow soft/fetch knots of spring then eager morning."

It's almost as if, because of its inability to engage, the separated body can detect a greater subtlety in the absences of perception. In this case she is attuned to both the physical manifestation of time ("knots") and the *feeling* of time ("eager") in the motion of spring.

Throughout the sections "Digestibles of the Sun" and "Insomniac of a Zen-Garden Fruit," the shortest in the book, the images of childhood, natural landscapes and marriage presented all along in earlier sections recur and recur as if in waves. One is reminded of the genderedness of certain experiences: in a book written by and in the interchange and exchange between two female bodies, climaxes may be multiple ones.

The penultimate sequence, "Photovoltaic," does indeed "turn" in "light"; it turns from a pure climactic moment of lingual ecstasy to an earnest injunction to "Write poems/starve off death."[56] It continues to alternate between an address to an outside "Lord" and later "you," and an internal observational voice. The "you" shifts and changes throughout the sequence, and unlike—for example—in Louise Glück's *The Wild Iris* (another work which deals with the traffic between human and divine in which the speaker of the poems alternate among flowers, gardener and god), here it is harder to say (or perhaps better to say the question is irrelevant) who the "you" in any given poem is: a human addressee, the "Lord" or divine element or the speaker herself (herselves!).

It's appropriate to have that level of confusion for a poem that in its first line seems to use the phrase "wild cherry" as a verb.[57]

> Lord let me all I can wild cherry
> I'm dazed all my ways of arriving bear tracks
> failure of being torn to pieces is me
> mumbling anxiety and I love my heart

"Dazed" indeed, the supplicant finds in this poem her path intersected not only with "bear tracks" (animal beings) but also "dew stars," and the earth in repeated iterations. The ecstatic uncoupled language she actually refers to as "vernacular"— not the heightened and ritualistic language of prayer with its human hierarchy of entry (priesthood, scholarship, etc.) and its imagined divine hierarchy of reception (who is worthy or washed clean enough for prayer, whose prayers will actually be answered, etc.)—but rather the plain speech of those "uneducated," the perhaps always "unwashed!"

The vernacular is confused, stumbles along (note the inverted subject in line 3), and moves against the linearity of address expected in a prayer designed for communal worship. No "mass" here but individual address, moreover not even between supplicant and "God" but between two human women who declare:

> I do each day lightly suffering desire
> for kindness vividly today
> idiot red unselfish green blue threadbare of cloud
> outside the labyrinth imagining my life

The "idiot" or wise person again makes an appearance here suffering, though lightly, desire. The scintillation of colors seems to belie this suffering; though threadbare or not she is still engaged in the highest form of praise, "imagining." The labyrinth, place of confusion and even danger, is abandoned here, and threads—*sutras* or sacred texts, threads the devoted tie around their wrists, threads made to weave tapestries or laws, threads that prisoners can use to escape said labyrinths—all flutter away in the stuttering music and assonance of the praising phrases.

Of course what priesthood, scholarship or institutions offer is precisely this: the *organization* of knowledge, and the "inside"-*insight* of achieved wisdom. When we say "received" knowledge we mean someone has collected it, passed it down, given it *to* us. But *who* has given it to us? The books of the bible were voted on and included based on decisions of a council. A caliph ordered the writing down and binding of the oral document that was the Quran, and then of course he ordered it "ordered." All variant versions were collected and burned.

An ecstatic document, a document passed between two people from one mouth to another, would have to be comfortable with its variants, its impermanence. Of course, as I mentioned before, the two published versions of *Sappho's Gymnasium* do differ textually in more than one way. I myself catalogued more than forty differences between the two texts, some small, some large. There were eighteen examples of stanzas and lines that were transposed and appear in different places in their section or in different sections, there were around fourteen new stanzas in the work that appeared in *Rave,* and about as many that were removed, not including the entire first section "Prayer-fields," which is not reprinted. Such differences do not seem to be of concern to the text itself—permanence doesn't have much to add to the seeking of a body for sensual or spiritual knowledge: "Insistent love I won't outlive the words I lamb into your mouth."[58]

At any rate, any text that uses both "wild cherry" and "lamb" as verbs is scripture I'll sign up for. And the text of the section of "Photovoltaic," alone out of all the other sections in the book, is unchanged in both of its appearances in print.

Whether or not permanence is at stake, it *is* a seeking: "Empty of shit the race is on," the poets urge:[59]

> empty of eyes made of wood with indifference
> don't you straighten it
> don't pretend your mouth is not on fire
> that stupidity bursts the needle

And then they urge:

> race for the oar light sleeps to dream
> travel through shining the ration before you
> for every hurt be my large palm
> Poetry

"Poetry," at the end is the rescuer then, from the hurt, from the mouth on fire, from the indifference, even from the animal panic of bowel expulsion in times of grave danger. And what is the danger here? Death of the body? Loss of knowledge? The poets who traffic in oral ecstasy are channeling Sappho, of course, but doesn't that precisely outline the problem: the woman who sang, tenth of the muses, whose work was strafed to scraps by sand and war and history. The ancient epic of blood and death and the fall of the city were lovingly tendered from hand to hand, but the songs in a woman's voice, the songs of love and the body and Aphrodite, they drift away . . .

So how then are we supposed to continue on our path? Not by learning the chapter and verse but by bringing into our *own* body the process itself for the searching. And for that you need a school of certain sort.

If one can actually learn to "write" or pronounce out the words oneself, to lamb them into the mouth of another, then perhaps one can "read" *anything* as a sacred text. "Bird is drunk inside me," the poets observe later.

The final and titular section "Sappho's Gymnasium" opens, like any good school, with a series of dicta. But these dicta are meant not to contain but to open wide possibilities for "misbehavior" for its rowdy rabble of students:[60]

> Outside memory worship never dies
> . . .

Torn mists the doves I will love

. . .

Light struts cannot be broken

Make praise populations will last

When the poets say "outside memory," they may mean "besides memory," but they may also mean that "memory worship," or a writing in and through the body, is the thing that never dies, the thing that connects the finite body (not really finite at all because made of the infinite undying matter of the universe which neither begins nor ends and only transforms) to the infinite condition of energy (not really infinite at all because subject to the conditions of all matter and antimatter—if space bends perhaps time does as well? And if time does then what *about* energy . . . ?).

Thus laced one to another in a spiral that does and undoes itself endlessly we have not necessarily "read" or "recite" but rather "remember" and "sing." Here follows then an epigraph of the curriculum itself, fittingly, as delineated in the notes of *Sappho's Gymnasium,* a fragment from the Headmistress herself:[61]

I have a young girl good as blossoming gold
her ephemeral face I have formed of a key
dearer than skylark homelands

The love for the girl is a portal into emotion more dear than even a "homeland." Of this power metaphor the poets outline what's really at stake: that human love, connection with another, is deeper than nation, than "home," a surer form of worship than any other. This fragment, by Sappho, enters into the stream of the poem, mixes with the words of Begley and Broumas seamlessly.

In this moment even the eros of the breakdown of linguistic structures starts to disappear. "Dutyfree dove seapitched Eleni," the poets sing to Helen, muse of ultimate beauty, "nectar your carafe seafounder."

Sappho and Eleni—Helen's Greek name—weave themselves into the fabric of Broumas and Begley's own words and in this way there seems a generosity of intent in the text. There is in the poems that follow a real commitment to connection, to actual communication, not solely utterance tossed out into the winds of the world. "Tongue I owe you," the poets say, and they mean both that the tongue is a recipient of a debt but also that the tongue itself *is* the debt that must be gifted to another. Spiritual and sexy at once indeed and in deed.

This form of rapt bodily attention has been arrived at by a long and careful exploration of the body and its possibilities. What happens when one rolls back knowledge of the intellect and seeks instead knowledge of the body and its senses:

Preumbilical eros preclassical brain

Preumbilical eros would be the one body literally inside the other even *before* the stage of separateness. This is eros not of separate bodies meeting each other skin on skin but swimming *inside* one another's sensory awareness. The preclassical brain is one unhindered by discipline or disciplines, that separation of knowledge that seeks also to problematize and alienate the human mind from the body's most significant physical processes: birth, sexual awakening, grief, ecstasy, beautiful age, death.

And what if life in its limbloosening sweetbitter hem of experience is the illuminated part, then death even after death is diffuse, unknowable and unknown? What if "we" (all part of the same source?) transfuse "ourself" *into* flesh from the unknowing state precisely to do what the body can do: learn and know and with each death carry back a little bit more of that understanding?

"Pansappho unscalp unfleece unscalpel unskin of flowers our kin," the poets sing next.[62] This line sings musically even somewhat more when one remembers that in the Greek Sappho's name has a hard "p" sound which precedes the "f" in the middle of her name and would properly be pronounced "Sapfo." When the poets wrote in their essay on the collaboration, "My skin is the volunteer cipher of your emotion," they are not speaking to an abstract other but to me actually. To you. Actually. They equals you equals me equals who.

And so how could I be surprised then when on the next page I found a short letter, written actually to me—six years before I met Broumas in New York City, when I still lived in Washington, DC, was working in social justice organizing and having panic attacks at my constricted and constricting life, before I had started on the path of poetry at all, she pronounced this verse out loud. And then how could I be surprised when six years later I read this book for the first time and missed it?

Not until late 2010, ten years after I read this book for the first time, longing for mentors who kept leaving me by geography or by death, did I suddenly come across the note, cast directly at me—*me*—from across time:[63]

Justice missed hyperventilates poet
Buddha vowel in Mohammed child dared cross
far from mother olivegroves father almonds
lyric sap of maple far from Lesvos

I am far from my sources, parental, spiritual and otherwise. I dream my way home. My consonants—the religion I was born with, the rules I learned, the body I inhabit—may be that of a "Mohammad Kazim" but my vowels—the breath that moves through them—are from Buddha, Krishna and from innumerable other places. There was a time in my life when I knew that far from my sources in every way—far from "God" and far from poetry—I would have to make everything up myself, in a language quite before unheard.

This is a book both individual and expansive, both immediately local and quite endless, as open as the wide southern Mediterranean. And why say anything at the end of the essay at all except pronounce more words from traveling; it seems the end of the known universe:[64]

In the dark before the candle
where the archetype takes our unconscious to build
this work is forever

Notes

1. Broumas, *Rave,* 361.
2. Barthes, qtd in Broumas, *Sappho's Gymnasium,* ix.
3. Merwin, qtd in Broumas, *S G,* xi.
4. Broumas, *SG,* 13.
5. Broumas, *SG,* 20–21.
6. Broumas, *SG,* 28.
7. Broumas, 37.
8. Broumas, 38.
9. Broumas, 40.
10. Broumas, 43.
11. Broumas, 46.
12. Broumas, 5.
13. Broumas, 47.
14. Broumas, 50.
15. Broumas, 52.
16. Broumas, 53.
17. Broumas, 57.
18. Broumas, 58–59.
19. Elytis, qtd in Brouas, viii.
20. Broumas, 62.
21. Homer, *The Odyssey,* 8.
22. Broumas, 65.
23. Broumas, 66.
24. Broumas, 70.
25. Broumas, 73.
26. Broumas, 77.
27. Broumas, 80.
28. Broumas, 81.
29. Broumas, 89.
30. Broumas, 90.
31. Broumas, 93.
32. Broumas, *Rave,* 362.
33. Broumas, *S G,* 94.
34. Broumas, 96.
35. Broumas, 98.
36. Broumas 105.
37. Broumas, 110.
38. Broumas, 111.
39. Broumas, 112.
40. Broumas, 113.

41. Broumas, 117.

42. Broumas, 118.

43. Broumas, *Rave,* 207.

44. Broumas, *S G,* 119.

45. Broumas, 124.

46. Broumas, 126.

47. Broumas, 127.

48. Broumas, 129.

49. Broumas, 133.

50. Jordan, 564.

51. Broumas, *S G,* 137.

52. Broumas, 138.

53. Broumas, 139.

54. Broumas, 146.

55. Broumas, 149.

56. Broumas, 162.

57. Broumas, 161.

58. Broumas, 167.

59. Broumas, 168.

60. Broumas, 171.

61. Broumas, 172. Alternate translations of this stanza of Sappho can be found on p. 89 of the Barnstone translation, p. 269 of the Carson translation and is number 17 of Mary Barnard's fragments.

62. Broumas, 177.

63. Broumas, 181.

64. Broumas, 183.

Poetry and Space

Taking pictures down from the walls is the hardest part of packing. You are going to leave a space you lived in and perhaps loved and go to another place. If you can erase all traces of yourself from a place—often to satisfy the terms of the lease and receive the full amount of your security deposit—then who *were* you that you could vanish *without a trace?* Often, after everything is packed and the boxes are loaded and we are ready to get on the road, I have to walk through the apartment room by room and say goodbye to the space. Say goodbye to the space? Or say goodbye the person who lived there.

Sometimes reading old poems while working on new work feels like this, that there is a version of me which haunts the space of the space, an other from the past who is and isn't me. Nearly ten years ago I wrote a sequence of poems on the figure of Miriam the Prophetess, sister of Moses. It was interesting to me at that time to think of the Jews wandering the desert without a place to call home; at the time houses were being demolished to make way for new roads or new Israeli settlements under the pretext of their not having building permits or electrical permits. The irony was not lost on my poetic imagination. The practice of home demolition continues to this day.

In time I moved away from the overtly political in poetry and also somewhat away from the "performed voice" in a certain way, such as writing "persona" poems or dramatic monologues, which at the time I had been firmly engaged in. I had sent some of these poems to Enid Dame, who was putting together an anthology about Miriam. Dame unfortunately passed away before the anthology was completed and I never thought about publishing those poems again, perhaps because I thought they were my youthful work. (Not much of a youth, I was twenty-eight when I wrote them; youthful in poetry). Very recently the journal *Bridges* contacted me and said they were going to publish a selection of the anthology in honor of Enid and could I send the text of the poem so they could include it. I wrestled with the idea of publishing work from so long ago—was it as good as what I was writing now? It was so different in style and aesthetic temperament, was it really mine anymore? And then again, what rights did I have over that younger version of myself who worked so earnestly and diligently on those seven poems, really the first poems I wrote?

I was traveling alone through the south of France in the summer of 2000. My cousin, who is French and had been with me in Cassis—the place at which the Alps drop into the sea and travel along the floor of the Mediterranean (they re-emerge briefly as Corsica and Sardinia) to Africa—had just left to return to Paris. I wanted to go to Corsica but had to wait four days before the boat I had passage on was leaving. I took myself to Arles—a place where city is piled on top of city—the Greek Arles, the Roman Arles, the medieval Arles, Van Gogh's Arles—each marked with tiles set into the center of the street.

The medieval city itself—pedestrian only—still stands, surrounded by its original wall. Around it a network of modern roads and neighborhoods. But inside the ancient and modern live happily together without conflict. A nearly perfect Roman coliseum has been unearthed near the center of town. That night I went to hear Natacha Atlas sing in the ancient open-air Greek amphitheater only a few blocks away.

When I went back to Marseille to catch the night boat I forgot to bring cash on board with me and forgot to order dinner for myself. There was no way to feed myself once the boat set sail. So hungry to the point of distraction I prowled the upper decks, watching the coast disappear into blue darkness. Eventually I did sleep and woke up in another country. I am still so intrigued by that image of the night boat—a vessel that takes you from one place to another without your participation, possibly even against your will; but your new condition of course is not escapable. I think sometimes of the spontaneous religious conversion that C. S. Lewis talked about. You are on a journey and then quite suddenly you are somewhere else, nothing like where you were, nothing like where you expected to be.

How strange it was to lose myself there without my cousin, the translator, to muddle through with half-phrases, spending most of my time by myself in silence, wandering from place to place just watching and looking. But who was I looking for? The poems I wrote started to condense themselves to smallest phrases without connective syntax from line to line. A couple of these poems, including "The City," "The Studio" and "Ruin" appear in my book *The Far Mosque*. It was hard to learn how to write a sentence with complex clauses again. Harder still to write a paragraph. I'm not quite sure that I've been able to master it, or then again if I ever had.

In the late summer of 2001 I moved from New York City north into the Hudson Valley. It's a place of intense spiritual power, strung up and down with monasteries, ashrams and Buddhist temples. When Swami Vivekananda, the man who first introduced vendanta and yoga philosophy to the West in the nineteenth century, settled in America, he moved to the mid-Hudson Valley, as did Swami Chinmayananda, author of the book *Self-Unfoldment*, and many other Hindu, Buddhist and Christian teachers and communities. Just ten days after I left New York City, the physical landscape of New York City changed as two buildings were knocked down by airplanes dropping from the sky, the emotional landscape changed—new willingness of anger, an acceptance of the absolute requirement of endless war—and even the landscape of language changed, new phrases suddenly coined to cope with our drastic new reality constructed from pre-fab materials by a group of people prepared for just such a situation: war on terror, orange alert, homeland security, nightmare phrases from dystopic science fiction suddenly embraced with nationalist passion.

Through the late autumn and into the winter of that year I wrote prodigiously into the new chaos that descended into the world. My sentences knit one to the other, but often without syntactic regularity or grammatical meaning. I found my poems tying themselves in knots the way poetry in Latin might—where word order is utterly flexible and meaning can be parsed out only with an understanding of verb declensions and noun cases. Since English unlike Latin does not have these sorts of constructions I found myself delighting in the unmeaning words could unmake; it didn't seem so wrong against the backdrop of a public discourse that completely turned words into shadows of themselves and phrases uttered in the evening news seemed completely disconnected from actuality.

During the years I spent in the valley, I was transfixed by the river. By the river I transfixed was. If the disappearing buildings in New York City could have actually affected the psyche of the citizenry (just try to imagine two mountains that once loomed over your town suddenly not being there anymore), the presence of the river, though two miles from where I lived, out of sight and out of hearing, still seemed to be an artery connecting me to some unnamable sources. It sank into me.

The Hudson River is an estuary system—the water flows out to the endless sea, but the sea also flows up the river to nearly where I was then living. I liked living in that place, the place where the river unmakes itself, dresses back into salt and origin, the place the water of the ocean reaches, where it then turns and returns.

I stayed along the river for years, moving south to Beacon, NY. The town lies between the great ridge of Mount Beacon on one side, nestling up to the river on the other side. I have always been haunted by the places where the mountains meet the shore—the stone coast of Maine, the island of Corsica, the northwest Oregon coast—and always imagined such as my dream-landscape. In the landscape of the dream I saw the paintings of Agnes Martin at the Dia:Beacon museum.

It was Martin who said two things about art that have stayed with me. First she said, regarding the idea of "form" in painting, "You wouldn't think of form at the ocean." I always understood this to mean Martin's dismissal of consideration of form as a quality of experience for either the painter or the viewer. But later she says, "I think of looking at one of my paintings as a crossing of the beach to get to the ocean."[1] Here Martin expresses a belief that the painting is merely a passage or portal to the ineffable experience. Form may or may not be present in the painting itself—certainly you could not argue that Martin herself was unconcerned with formal structures or approaches—but the exceptional level of emphasis is given to the viewing of the painting and all the context tied to it—where it is seen, and under what physical conditions. Martin's paintings have an exceptional home in the Dia museum where the surfaces themselves change in the natural light setting depending on the time of day you look at them, also the season, and also the climatic conditions of the sky outside.

There are other places in the museum that assume poetic space: up in the small exhibit space of the attic is a Louise Bourgeois installation consisting of a huge metal cage surrounded by the eight legs of a sinister spider. In the center of the cage an antique chair, its red pillow faded and threadbare. Just one flight down from there Fred Sandback's vacant and mysterious portals delineated by lines of yarn pulled taut, and another half flight down leads one to the hangar-sized room containing four room-sized sculptures by Richard Serra called "ellipses." Nowhere else in the building do you feel as keenly its former incarnation—a factory. "Museum" nearly everywhere else, here in the great former receiving bay you really can hear the sounds of the old machines, remember that you are in a place that used to be another place.

As I walked through the ellipses, the walls themselves curved up or down. Sometimes there would be less than a foot of walking space, but since the walls opened out toward the ceiling allowing light to flood into the narrow corridor one would not feel cramped at all. Then the dimensions reversed—the floor space became very wide, three feet, but the ceiling closed in—the space felt constrained, dark, threatening. One is walking through the metal corridor for what seems an impossibly long time when it finally opens out into a small chamber in the heart of the ellipse. There's nothing in space that will teach you or carry you. What do you do when you get to the ocean on the other side of the beach? What is the heart of the matter after all?

Is that all art is really good for? To lead you somewhere and leave you there?

Donald Revell says a poem is what's left behind after poetry has passed through a place.[2] I like that because it means you are always working toward a new awareness but I don't like that because it seems that there is no possibility of a transcendental moment of awareness and liberation. In yoga and meditation whenever you feel like you are having a moment of consciousness you are supposed to remind yourself "Not this. Not this."

Meaning that whatever you've experienced is just one more step on the road to bliss but not bliss itself. But at the heart of that denial is that there is, eventually, at the end of it, bliss.

Isn't there?

It all seems connected somehow to the question of whether or not Hagar panicked in the desert. She was alone with her infant son, Ismail, he was dying of thirst, and she ran back and forth between the mountains looking for water. In the Islamic story she is driven by panic. But if prayer itself is a form of mortal panic, maybe what happened to Hagar is beyond panic but rather the purest form of faith. She didn't even think to ask God for anything, she just bolted, against all reason and logic, looking in the desert for water.

Lucky for her Ismail's heels hammering the rock released a spring, called Zam-Zam. Hagar ran though there was no reason to run. Water came up at exactly the spot the baby needed it. In fact, she never noticed in the seven times she ran between the two hills looking for a spring that the baby had already turned his head to one side and drunk.

Zam-Zam still flows and provides water to the city of Makkah [Mecca] today. It's bottled and provided to pilgrims. My parents went to Makkah on Hajj about ten years ago and brought me back two bottles of this water. I am not sure if you are supposed to save it, or pray for something very particular with it. I drank a bottle just to taste its spirit. I cannot remember if I offered a prayer, and if I offered a prayer I cannot remember what it was. The other I still have.

But I have a problem with prayer. Is it panic or in the most perverse way an actual denial of faith? One night a year, in the brand of Shi'a Islam my family practices, we are allowed to write notes to the twelfth Imam, Imam Mahdi, who is supposed to be in occlusion, utterly and unfiguratively alive and aware of worldly events and waiting until the time is right to make his reappearance. We write notes of our most ardent wish and then we are supposed to drop the letters into running water at the midnight hour. The last year I did it—nearly seven years ago, when my wish was most ardent I found myself unable to choose, unable to write. Finally I did the most alarming thing I could do in a note to the Imam, the most alarming thing anyone could do in a prayer to a divine authority—I gave the man a choice. I wrote to him, "quench my desire or change the rules that disallow it," unable even in the most extremely hermetic act to say what I really wanted.

So how does a poem work then in the pressure of that simultaneous desire to keep a secret and to tell everything?

I went in the fall of 2004 on a trip with my students from the Culinary Institute of America to visit the farms, restaurants, wineries and processors in Northern California. In the first half of the trip we toured various farms in the Salinas area and our guide explained to us that the reason the area was rich and fertile was that there was a subterranean river flowing through the ground eight hundred feet below. The submerged desire transforms the landscape into bounty that provides produce for a hundred million people or more.

A hundred miles to the north and a week and a half later we were in Sonoma County, deep in the caverns of a champagne producer listening to the story of how the technique of hand-turning the bottles of champagne to eliminate sediment was being transferred to new and sophisticated machines. The wine-producing regions of Northern California have such rich and intensely productive soils for wine grapes because each of them—Napa Valley and Sonoma Valley—were once in turn the ocean floor. As the plates of the earth moved first one then the other was shoved against the continent and surged above the water to become dry land.

On the grounds of a winery, on a slope leading up into the hills surrounding the vineyards, there is a rough frame with a door in it, doorpost and lintel, not attached to any structure. Next to it in clear lettering is a helpful sign: Door Leading Nowhere.

I'd like my work to lead me to blankness. I'd like blankness to lead me to my work. Having been lost and alone or unsure so much in my life, it pleases me to think, as Fanny Howe has written, of "bewilderment" as a locus for spiritual evolvement or advancement. It seems to me in poems that the underground keeps emerging to become dry land and that there is perhaps a new underground. And as Mahmoud Darwish has taught us, or as anyone in Beirut, Baghdad or New York City knows, cities do disappear, buildings and mountains both can indeed collapse.

I live now nowhere. I commute to a workplace in Central Pennsylvania in a valley carved horizontally by the ice age in a town founded as a basis to tame the frontier and re-educate the people found there. The central intersection of Carlisle is Hanover and High Streets where Benjamin Franklin famously first met the Indian chiefs to negotiate a settlement. It is very odd, as a different kind of Indian, to live in the place where the first series of promises were made that would undo entire nations.

Even my own body is a space I do not own; three times in New York City at a weekend conference, I was mistaken for another Indian poet who does not resemble me in the least. He is a half a foot taller, broader, just a little darker, and much more effusive and socially engaging than I am (Ravi's natural resting face smiles while I always look like I am trying to remember something). The last of these times I was mistaken by someone I had met before and knew. She introduced me to her husband as the wrong somebody and I was so taken aback and unsure about exactly how not to embarrass this person by insisting on myself that somehow, without planning it, I found myself playing along. We all made about ten seconds of small talk about *Drunken Boat,* the on-line journal Ravi edits, and about the school he teaches at and then I politely excused myself.

Walking away from the encounter I was shocked at myself, startled that I had so easily slipped out of my own body and life and into someone else's. I'd always imagined that poetry insisted on itself and that it would help me insist on my tricky body, raised in Islam but turning in all of its complicated desires another way. But there I was on the 1 train, rattling uptown, in another man's body, a Hindu man, married with a child, wondering if it was a pure colonization or if he, somewhere else in the city that same moment, had just been mistaken for me.

What on earth could have possessed me to decide, on the third transport out of myself, to suddenly decide to no longer fight it—to just make social conversation, anything to get out of having to say one more time, "Actually I'm Kazim Ali." It's not so hard to change your name, or have your name changed.

After all, what would it be like then to drop this malleable identity and slip into his: waking up in another country, taller, stronger, turned into a charming man known to many people, coupled to a woman—quite suddenly finding that the conditions of my body's flowering and self-realization were no longer illegal according to the laws of my parents' religion?

I'm in love with the place I live in New York City right now even if it takes a long time to get there from anywhere. Marble Hill is a funny neighborhood in the Bronx which isn't really in the Bronx. It's the very northern tip of the island of Manhattan, even past Inwood. Formerly bordered on the north by the twisting Spuyten Duyvil Creek, Marble Hill is a vibrant neighborhood crossed through by one-way streets strategically arranged to make it impossible to drive through on your way to somewhere else.

Somewhere at the end of the nineteenth century, the city decided to make the waterway less complicated for ships traveling to Manhattan's Upper East Side and blasted a canal through the island at the northern end of Inwood. Marble Hill had become an island and remained that way for nearly twenty years when the creek was filled in and it became part of the Bronx geographically though politically remains part of the borough of Manhattan. It appears floating in space on the other side of the river on maps of Manhattan. No one really knows what to do with it—the phone company and the post office call it the Bronx but the New York State Supreme Court rules it on paper Manhattan.

What is it like to have laws written down on paper that can only approximate spiritual truth and daily material realities? How can you explain to people where you live when you are not on any maps or on all the wrong maps, and besides that how can you explain to people how to get to where you are when all the streets run one-way the wrong way and you wear another man's name?

One condition of living nowhere and having two homes in different cities is that you put things down on the nightstand in one city and try to pick them up in another. It's one thing when you lose toothbrushes, books, shoes, passports or checkbooks, but quite something else when you lose a folder of poems—forty pages of them, first drafts, not typed up in the computer. It happened last summer, somewhere between a writing retreat in Virginia, my sister's wedding in Buffalo and a trip to Maine. I put the folders down in one city and when I went to pick them up in the other they were not there.

I had to carry them around in my memory, thinking and thinking before I could write some lost lines down. Some of them restored themselves, but most of them are drifting into the wind like the novel Apu tossed into the valley from the mountaintop at the end of the *Aparajito*. He's spent the whole film writing it and you never do get to read it.

My poems themselves are hiding somewhere, under a box in someone's house, cleared away from the hotel table by the cleaning staff, misplaced in the pocket of an airplane seat, left at a coffee shop—they've vanished. They don't exist anymore. One poet friend suggested I write to the absence itself, the implacable place.

If traveling seems like an apt metaphor for the transport poetry can provide, it's important to remember that for some of us, it is still fraught with actual danger and serves as a very effective reminder that we are still always strangers and threats. I have not traveled in the last five years without waiting for half an hour or longer at the ticket counter, my passport taken away into the back office and examined. I'm paperless there, no one, a hair's breadth away from losing everything—my rights, my job, my rage, while phone calls are made to ascertain I am who I say I am. On one occasion I was asked to give the website for the university I told them I worked at. On another day a sympathetic agent, looking over her shoulder first, whispered to me that I should think about changing my name since my legal name on the passport (Mohammad K. Ali) was the thing that was triggering the background checks. "They are looking for someone that has the same name as you," she confided in me. They will not have to look hard to find someone with my legal name, equivalent in some countries with "John Smith."

On only one occasion was I singled out and taken into the enclosure. The officer told me I had a right to have the curtains pulled around me for privacy. I declined, wanting to make sure his actions were seen. There the young man patted me down, giving me a running narration while he did it: "I'm touching your stomach, I'm going to touch your crotch, I will use only the back of my hand, I'm touching your thigh . . ." When he had finished I sat down to put my shoes back on and put my glasses on and found myself crying. We imagine we are independent and strong people, we imagine we would have righteous anger in such a situation, but we don't. We don't own our bodies, we certainly don't own what others will think of them, and we have no right to our own rage—any glimmer of expression of it would result in firmer and harsher treatment.

We are supposed to forget our own bodies, forget their rage, their humiliations, the disastrous ways they can fail us; we are supposed to believe the spirit is superior to the flesh, transcends; we are supposed to believe that the spirit is eternal while the mortal flesh disappears. Honestly it horrifies me I do not look more tenderly at this beautiful incarnation, this creature that is walking with me, that the intellect and the spirit do not recognize how much of our wisdom comes from the body, our hope, our magnificence.

When we hear about the war, we are not supposed to imagine it happening to actual bodies. And if the bodies are actual, they should be foreign bodies. No soldiers' bodies would be seen; even photographs of their flag-draped coffins could be considered obscene and in poor taste. How do we occupy any space at all when awareness of the individual body is so suppressed and denied and for the crassest of political purposes?

One of the reasons *The Iliad* is so political is that it does tell about the individual soldier's bodies. Whenever someone is killed the poet recites not only the often grisly and graphic anatomical details of their deaths, but frequently also gives an account of their families, their lineage and offspring, description of their homelands or properties, usually ending with a description of the moaning spirit fleeing shrieking into the underworld. Reading page upon page of such description really gives one a new understanding of the horror of public war visited on the individual body and family.

But what if you have no homeland? What if you come from nowhere? What if you are divorced from ancestry by your lifestyle and by choice or not by choice childless? Like many of us I was born in one place, grew up in another, went away to college in another, started my life in another. Like a few others I repeated the cycle: returned home, went away to college again, started my life again. I still go from one place to another though this time by choice.

Returning home to my Pennsylvania apartment one day, in the cold of winter at the end of the semester, late on a Monday night, I turned the key in the lock and opened it looking into the apartment beyond, left in a state of half-occupancy: a book was open on the table, a cup of half-drunk coffee beside it, a towel draped over the back to the kitchen chair, some crumbs from toast on the table. The comforter on the bed was pulled back and there were two pairs of shoes lined up next to the door. For a minute or two I hesitated there at the threshold, wanting very much to enter from the cold, dimly aware that I could, yet in my conscious mind waiting for someone to appear, to give me permission, so unsure was I of who lived there.

Notes

1. Martin, 7.
2. Revell, *Invisible Green,* pp. 27–28. I am paraphrasing his argument.

Poetics of G-D

To me a poem begins itself in silence and, as at the eye of the storm, there is dead calm, there is a dark place in every poem about which no one can speak.

In this same fashion, the mosque in which Muslims worship is empty, God Himself has no actual name. I am not sure you can say the thing itself but can only illuminate the search for it, tell the story of a process toward understanding.

Poems have a linguistic energy but an inner spiritual energy as well. Some people call it breath.

The difference between the outside meaning of the poem and the subterranean depth is that of consonants to vowels. One of them you can learn about and practice with your mouth, the other has to proceed directly from the interior, from animal instinct or divine engine, who can say?

But you need both of them to speak.

The Rose Is My Qibla

Sohrab Sepehri's Journey East

When my father went to Iran to work, he wanted to know what to bring back for me. Other than his voice, I wondered, whispering again the *adhan* into my ears?

Poetry, I told him, bring me poetry. He brought me several books of contemporary Iranian poets translated into English, among them a couple of short books by Sohrab Sepehri. The translations were rough, but through the words I *felt*, in another language, one I didn't know, the reach of Sepehri toward understanding.

Growing up, my father recited to us Urdu poetry, Arabic verses, sometimes Farsi. The sounds live nestled in my ear with the echoes of my daily prayers. But I wandered—a Muslim of queer disposition and yogic leanings, wandering and wondering between Vedanta and Sufi teachings, always not-knowing, always happily not-found.

Sohrab Sepehri was trained as a painter. He traveled frequently around the world, including to East Asia, Europe and the United States of America. In 1964 and 1965 he took a long trip through China and Japan, learning about Buddhism while studying woodworking and painting. On his way back to Iran he stopped in India for several months. Upon his return home he wrote a rapturous poem called "Water's Footfall," a "lyric-epic" as influenced by Islam and Sufi philosophy as it is by the Buddhist and Hindu philosophies and beliefs Sepehri was exposed to during his journey.

"I am a Muslim," Sepehri declares, early in the poem, but then goes on to clarify:[1]

I am a Muslim:
The rose is my *qibla*.
The stream my prayer-rug, the sunlight my clay tablet.
My mosque is the meadow.
I rinse my arms for prayers along with the thrum and pulse
of windows.
Through my prayers streams the moon, the refracted light of
the sun.
Through translucent chapters I look down at the stones in
the stream-bed.

Every part of my prayer is clear straight through.

Sepehri is at home in the natural world, the world that exists, and his God is not bodiless nor remote, but incarnate in every piece of matter and as close as the nearest living thing. When Muslims pray we pray in the direction of the Ka'aba in Mecca. This direction—designated in hotels in the Islamic world by a golden arrow imprinted on the ceiling—is called the *qibla*. In the earliest days of Islam, this *qibla* was toward the Far Mosque in Jerusalem, but after the Prophet's *mehraj,* or "night-journey," the *qibla* was changed to the Near Mosque, the Ka'aba.

Abraham and his son Ishmael built the Ka'aba on the site supposedly marking the place where Adam and Eve entered the earth. They used as a cornerstone a rock Ishmael had brought with him—called later in the *zubuur* of David "the stone that the Builder refused." Called "the black stone," it marks the place at the Ka'aba where devoted pilgrims are to begin their prescribed circumambulations of the mosque. The Ka'aba is an entity fixed—for millennia—at the heart of Mecca and at the heart of Islam. But nothing is fixed—not locality, not divinity—for Sepehri. He writes:

My Ka'aba is there on the stream-bank,
in the shade of the acacia trees.
Like a light breeze, my Ka'aba drifts
    from orchard to orchard, town to town.

My black stone is the sunlight in the flowers.

This experience of rapture floods the long prose lines of the poem, which begins in a poetic autobiography recounting the death of the poet's father, his experiences dealing with grief and doubt, and then growing up and leaving home: "I saw a man down at heels going door to door asking for canary songs, I saw a street cleaner praying, pressing his forehead on a melon rind."[2]

This conflation of ordinary things, discarded things, with the spiritual and divine seems to suffuse the poem. The small clay tablet upon which Shi'a Muslims press their foreheads when they pray is usually made not of melon rind, but of sacred clay taken from the earth at Karbala, Iraq, the place at which Imam Hussain, grandson of Prophet Mohammed, was killed by his political rivals in the Damascus Caliphate. But here, the regular institutions of knowledge do not suffice. If Sepehri seems Sufi in inclination it is the Sufism of Rabi'a or Lalla, pure devotion that appeals; the institutions of learning and fixity the poet can do without:

> On the desperate scholar's bedside table a whole jug
>   brimming with questions.
> I saw a mule bent under the burden of student essays.
> A camel slung with empty baskets of proverbs and axioms.
> A dervish stumbling under the weight of his *dhikr*.

But everything in his spiritual search is not sunlight and melon rinds though. There is a real danger, Sepehri seems to point out, in resisting the natural urge toward union:[3]

> A crack in the wall flights off the persistent advances
>   of the sunlight.
> Stairs struggling against the Sun's long leg.
> Loneliness fights the song.
> Pears ache to fill the empty basket.
> Pomegranate's jewel-seeds refusing to burst
>   under the teeth's insistence.

> [. . .]
> Forehead presses down against the cold clay prayer tablet.

Mosque tiles unpeel from the walls,
　　flying toward defenseless worshipers.
　　[. . .]
Butterfly-army takes on the Pest Control Program.
Dragonfly-swarm versus Water Main Workers.
Regiments of calligraphy brushes storm the printshop
　　to assault the leaden font letters.
Poetry clogs up the throat of the poet.

Not only is a worshiper laying his forehead on an actual clay tablet (rather than, for example, a melon rind) equated with other examples of failure, but the worshipers inside an actual mosque (unlike those frolicking in the meadow, for example) have something real to fear! (Let me point out that this poem was published in 1964, a little before the image of the tiles unraveling from a mosque's dome to kill the worshipers inside became actual tragic reality.) In other skirmishes the butterflies and insects and calligraphy pens actually take on and take down the instruments of "civilization."

Mohammad Jafar Mahallati explains, "Sepehri's abstract and meditative idiom, which made him subject to severe criticism of leftist political activists before and during the Iranian revolution, has become very popular in Iran today exactly because his unconventional gnostic approach to language defies the official rhetoric of political religion. Therefore and quite ironically he has gained far more relevance to the current social dynamics of Iran than the literature produced by his critics three decades ago."[4]

In another litany, the natural world and the devoted poet do not fare so well:[5]

A baby's rattle murdered on the mattress.
A story killed at the alley-opening of sleep.
Sorrow executed by order of song.
Moonlight shot at command of neon-lit night.
Willow tree strangled by order of the government.
Desperate poet murdered by a snowdrop flower.

The poet is seeking to find his place in the world and is not naïve about the complications of so doing. He knows that the world of order, the civilized world of timetables and train schedules and commerce, is not the same as the poetic world, the world of devotion and ecstasy. Repeating the poem's opening lines, he clarifies: "From Kashan I am but/there I was not born./I have no place of origin, no home./With fevered devotion/I built a house on the far side of night."

He knows, even though there is difficulty, he is on the side of wildness and mystery: "I have never seen two spruce trees at war./Never seen the willow subletting its shade to the earth./The elms offer their branches to the crows rent-free." He knows that through a real embrace of these converging life-giving forces an individual human can truly experience the richness of the world:[6]

> Let's eat bread and mallow flowers for breakfast.
> Let's plant a sapling in the lilt and pitch of each line.
> Let's sow silence between each syllable.
>
> Ignore all the storm-free books and the book
>   in which the dew is not wet
>   [. . .]
> We don't want the fly to be buffeted by the hands of the
>   wind.
> We don't want the tiger to pass through Creation's door
>   and disappear.
> Without the worm, we would be hollow.
> Repeal all the laws of trees if they deny the slithering
>   caterpillar.
> What would our clenching hands hold on to if there was no
>   death?

The closing of the poem sheds all of his doubts. He's desperate after all, to soak himself in the rain, to "take the pulse of the flowers," and to come to terms, once and for all, with Death.

He writes:[7]

> Let's not be in dread of death.
> Death is not the end of the dove or pigeon, or the cricket.
> Death fills the thoughts of the acacia trees.
> Death dwells pleasant in the mind's meadows.

Death recounts the story of Dawn to the townsfolk at night.
Death slides inside my mouth when I eat the sunwarm grape.
Death quivers inside the voice-box of the robin.
Death inked that calligraphy on the butterfly's wings.
Death sometimes harvests basil, drinks vodka,
     sits in the shade watching.
Every deep breath is filled with the air of Death.

And so the poet is left with an awareness of both sides of life, but
also aware that the human intellect is not equipped to under-
stand the spiritual mysteries of existence and that only without
poetic faculties can one hope to truly live:[8]

Let's let Loneliness sing its song, write a poem,
     go out into the streets.
Let's forget about everything.
Forget everything when at the bank teller's window
     and when lounging under the sycamore.
Our mission is not to unpetal the Rose's layered secret.
Maybe our mission is to float, drunk on the mystery of the
     Rose.
Let's pitch our tents on the other side of the hill from
     Knowing.
Wash our hands in the leaf's green ecstasy and prepare the
     picnic.
Let's be reborn when the sun dawns.
Let's unleash everything and water the flowers and windows,
     our understanding of space, sound and color.

Let's stitch Heaven between the two syllables of Being.
Fill and refill our lungs with eternity.
Unload the swallow of its burden of Knowledge.
Let's strip all the names from the clouds, sycamore,
     mosquito, summer

Let's climb up the wet blue rungs of rain higher and higher
     into Love

Let's open all the doors to every being, to sunlight,
     to the green trees and gardens,
to the dragonflies and cicadas and other winged things

> Maybe our real mission is to run between
> the lotus flower and the century, hunting
>   for some lingering echo of truth . . .

In the end, Sepehri created a haunting epic of the individual spirit's journey, informed by wild surrealism as well as a Sufi sensibility. The Hindu or Vedantic sense of death as a transformation or a realization haunts the text as do Zen and Buddhist ideas about the interconnectedness of all things.

Philosopher Soursh Dabbagh explains that Sepehri's "inclination towards more abstract thoughts subjected him to criticism by his contemporary literary critics such as Shamloo, Barahani, and Ashoori, who accused him of being disconnected from the social turbulences of 1970s in Iran."[9] Furthermore, as Mohammad Jafar Mahallati explains, "Sepehri's lines and images have entered the public consciousness in Iran to an extent that may seem odd to the American reader. Sepehri's poems are an important source of slang used increasingly in modern colloquial Persian. His combination of very simple diction with extremely dense layers of meaning provides a critical means to address sensitive social issues in a language that satisfies the Iranian poetic sensibility while negotiating the current social and political reality there; it requires subtlety of expression sometimes rather than boldness."[10]

Where before he dreamed of sowing silence, by close of "Water's Footfall," it is Heaven itself he is stitching into the words of existence. Leaving "Knowing" and "Knowledge" behind (which, interestingly enough, here belongs to the birds and donkeys and goats but not to humans), he wishes like Gertrude Stein to peel names away from the things in the world so we can experience them anew without the burden of past association. This too is an idea drawn directly from the Yoga Sutras of Patanjali, the idea that humans can achieve clear perception only by union with the divine.

What were only lotus seeds earlier in the poem have bloomed into flowers and, rather than a point of revelation themselves they are, like the Black Stone, only the beginning of a journey that—like Hagar in legend running seven times between the hills of Safa and Marwa in her impossible panic-driven search for water in the desert—the poet must enter his poem to undertake.

Notes

1. Sepehri, 13.
2. Sepehri, 16.
3. Sepehri, 18.
4. Sepehri, 9.
5. Sepehri, 19.
6. Sepehri, 23.
7. Sepehri, 24.
8. Sepehri, 25.
9. Quoted in Sepehri, 8.
10. Introduction to *The Oasis of Now: Selected Poems by Sohrab Sepehri,* translated by Kazim Ali and Mohammad Jafar Mahallati, BOA Editions, 2013..

Yoga and the Cessation of the Self

Breathe. Breathe, and the earth will open. I was taught this by my own body, hovering at the edge of disaster in my first yoga class ever, in Provincetown, a small village at the end of a peninsula flung into the ocean, the summer of 1999, in ruins. I'd left Washington, DC, two years earlier, left friends, my career, my life, a lover, and for the next two years just *hovered*—hovered because I had no direction to turn in, imagine that the compass was spinning like crazy or that the game pieces had been upset, were rolling in all directions.

Yet there, there on a yoga mat, sitting at the very front edge of a meditation cushion, rolling on the front of my sitting bones, drawing my belly in and up, I hovered—the torso is connected to the pelvis structurally only by four simple vertebrae bones—I hovered and then—

Then I let go.

What can I say here without sounding melodramatic? I expected to fall. I expected that everything I let go would be lost. I did not expect I would be caught. I would be held. I would be carried up. By only my own breath.

Imagine it. Practice it now if you want to. At the end of the exhale you can do nothing more or less than breathe in again. It's not quantum physics, nor karmic science, nor yogic philosophy. It's the involuntary function of the body. To flood itself with breath.

"Yoga is a discipline of tenderness for and awareness of the body," writes Reetika Vazirani in her essay "The Art of Breathing," "heart, lungs, kidney, pressure points to the inner life of the eye, third eye, eye of the spleen."[1] And it's tenderness I feel for myself that day in that class. At the end of the class, after ninety minutes of stretching, breathing, heart-opening, and spine-lengthening, we lay out in the "final rest" posture, called "corpse pose."

Because in every practice, there is a death of that practice, a moment at which one must return to one's life, and be in it. The point is what happens when you return from the practice? Has it taught you to be more human? As I lay there, so open, blood rushing to all the lonely places, my heart seemed open—really open—and from horizon to horizon of my life I felt all right. We turned over onto our right sides and drew our knees close to our chest in a fetal position, supposedly only for a moment before we gently pushed ourselves up to a sitting position. But I stayed. And what was beneath the sweet calm, hovering *just underneath* like the water in the earth wells up after a storm: welled up. And I wept. For all the choices I couldn't make, for the dark anger I had for myself that had hidden beneath my heart as hard as a fist, for the hopes and imagined future that had scattered and were lost.

What do we tell a child when it cries too fiercely? Or what do we tell our friend who is about to lose their cool? We say just this: breathe. Breathe.

Breath brought me back to myself and in the fall of that year I moved to New York City. While I was there I signed up for the first yoga class I found. Why did I do such thing? What was my "attachment" to yoga? Was I hoping it would make me strong and sleek? Help me to deal with stress? Secretly, I felt it was a "solution" to the empty feeling I had. Yoga was going to save me, I believed. Secretly I imagined that the bliss experience I'd had that summer was a genuine window into my true self—a window that I might open again and again with a consistent yoga practice.

Is it any wonder that I might come to see my relationship to yoga as analogous to my relationship to poems? They too were the most secret and powerful of recipes. They were, sometimes it seemed, all I had going for me. They were the closest things to my heart, the things I could never explain, and the things that could never somehow explain me. My seeking that bliss window, that secret room, in yoga, helped me immeasurably when I confronted the blank page or the blank mind in the writing of poems.

In fact, in those years, I barely remember ever having what's called "writer's block." If I could breathe, I could listen to the sound of my breath. If I could listen to the sound of my breath, I could measure the sounds of the world against it. If I could measure the sounds of the world against the sound of my own breath, then of course I could discern what lay between those two things: words. Which were only sounds after all, and sounds only breath.

"Do you know where Allah is?" asked Hassan Al-Askari, the eleventh Imam of Shi'a faith. "Listen: He is closer to you than even your breath."

In November of 2001, after I had left New York, I went back to Provincetown and attended a weekend workshop with Olga Broumas. In her workshop description Broumas said she would guide us in "relaxing through the breath and voice into [']not knowing,['] following the sound into words, then fragments or phrases, which slowly bring us into the warm awareness of what we didn't know we knew." This idea of the breath as a great primeval ocean, that our experiences and memories are ancient and still within us, that they surface, and submerge, resurface . . .

All the weaknesses and the hard parts, the anger that coagulated into a fist, still in me? That bliss moment, the weeping, the release of pain back into the ocean, still in me? "Still" means anyhow a condition of the past carried into the present. Also means a place of calmness—to be still. To be "still" means to be present. To be "present" then means to carry all of the past conditions "still in me."

We spent the weekend together with Broumas, sometimes practicing for long periods a ritual silence, other times chanting wordless syllables together, other times willfully pronouncing the vowels of our names without the constraining consonants. One student, said, "My name is Jason Zuzga. I'm hemmed in by consonants." "But, oh," Broumas declared in her voice of the wide open sea, "in Greek your name is Ia-so-nas . . ." dragging out the long vowels of the name. So for the rest of the weekend Jason became *Iasonas* to all of us. We were asked to say our name in our mother's voice so the others could repeat it back to us. How grateful I was to hear my name—Kaah-zim—said over and over again properly without the hundreds of mutilated variations I grew up hearing.

It seems such a simple thing to say one's own name. Perhaps in order to write about our individual experience in the world, we first need to find our way back through the layers of socialization and assimilation and acculturation, back to our primeval strangenesses, back to the place where breath body unspool the words from the meanings and the vowels unmoor from their consonants. Didn't Rumi go mad with grief and rave like a lunatic when his friend, his love, his Shams disappeared into the night?

Broumas taught us about "ecstasy": in the original meaning of that word, to be "standing outside" one's self—to literally lose one's identity, but to do this by releasing attachment to the individual ego, release selfish attachment to only the world one perceives, and attach again to a larger spirit, attach to the universal world exactly how it truly exists beyond individual perception. Tell me again how easy it is to see yoga and meditation practice as a metaphor for your writing of poems?

When I first came across reference to "The Art of Breathing" in which fellow Indian poet and yogi Reetika Vazirani wrote about her love of yoga, I became ecstatic. I wanted to read this essay and understand how this writer described the experience that for so long I had felt unable to describe. Perhaps I could learn from her why, after so many years of yoga practice and so many pages and pages and pages of writing, I felt no closer to being able to embrace the moments of my life, and felt no closer to writing the truthful, visceral, beautiful, musical poems I wanted to be able to write. "Your tongue is tired of saying/sacred words over and over//and your fingers, you've worked them/to the nub copying texts," sang Lalla, "but the rage stored inside you/has found no way to leave."[2]

Indeed Vazirani's essay begins at a point so familiar to me, the point of mispronunciation and alienation. "My yoga instructor, Jennifer," Vazirani's essay opens, "is a white woman from Virginia. I am the only East Indian in the class."[3] The students in Vazirani's yoga class who mispronounce all the Sanskrit names, the receptionist at her doctor's office who calls her "Retinka Varzeenee," all feel familiar to me.

But the essay itself is not the one I expected. Vazirani barely discusses the actual "art of breathing" of yoga and instead takes the reader back in time from the starting place of her yoga mat and the oddness of being taught yoga by a white woman, back to her upbringing in the DC area, and to the cultural and religious practices of her household. Vazirani's essay seemed more about her problematic relationship to her culture than an exploration of how yogic breath came into the writing of her poems. When Vazirani does return to a description of the actual breathing practice, it is not in connection with her personal yoga practice, nor her writing practice, but rather to her childhood memory of her father's practice of "oamkar"—breathing deeply and chanting the syllable "Om" over and over again.

There is a belief that this syllable "Om" is the sound of the whole universe. In chanting it one certainly feels the whole universe could fit inside. The torso opens, the side-ribs open, the mouth and throat open, and sound fills the body. If there was a Big Bang is it possible that the residual echo that scientists have heard bouncing back from the end of the universe is only the sound of Om? Vazirani sits with her father, "trying to match him breath for breath."

What can be quite disconcerting is the lack of transitions. I finally feel like I have arrived at what will be the point of "Art of Breathing" when she moves on, without carrying the idea any further, to her father's suicide on Father's Day several years later.[4] With a devastating sentence—"The death of my father is for me the beginning of my distrust for yoga."—Vazirani makes a break from her subject of breathing and turns instead to her increasingly problematic relationship to her Indian culture throughout her young adulthood.

But the suicide—and the disconcerting present tense construction of the sentence (". . . *is* for me the beginning . . .)— rest uneasily at the heart of her essay. The essay itself breathes around that small core: not just the actual suicide of Sunder Vazirani, but Reetika's brief recounting of it, the family's silence. Reading the essay now, that true subject embedded within its avowed subject is a silence that deafens. Because I know now, years after Reetika wrote the essay, that no matter what resolution she comes to in it is going to fall short. Breathing didn't save her. Her poetry didn't save her. Yoga didn't save her.

It wasn't until some months later, when I read Vazirani's book *World Hotel*, that I could see how breath and yoga practice had entered her work. In "The Art of Breathing" Vazirani describes breath in her own body, "The heat in my body leads me to spaces within myself, as if to rooms in a house I had never let myself fully inhabit. I can enter deep and secret rooms, light and dark rooms—spaces between my vertebrae and the warm pouch of my pancreas." Throughout the poems of *World Hotel*, one can feel the syntax and line breaks shifting across sentences and musical units to create in the reader some of that breath music that only a regular practitioner of *pranayama* could compose. Read this last stanza of the poem "Seeta" out loud to yourself:[5]

> I was the orphan Seeta. And the mother of.
> That is over. I am tired.
> I think, sunshine on ships
> when I traveled, laughs on Malabar Hill—
> my life did not comprise me it was so brief.

"Yoga aims to banish ignorance," she writes in "The Art of Breathing," "in order to achieve serenity [. . .] It is a long road."[6] But where can such a long road lead? One hopes, as does Vazirani, it leads to "happiness/peace/compassion." Only here it didn't. Here it instead led, despite breath, despite practice and generosity of spirit, to desperation, to immense grief, to fatal and final action—the death of Vazirani along with her young son in the summer of 2003.

Rita Dove, one of Vazirani's mentors, has said, "This was not the Reetika you knew. At that moment she was truly insane. She couldn't find her way back to herself."[7] Vazirani writes at the end of her essay about her yoga teacher from Virginia with a candid admission, "Somebody like her might have helped my father, who in the end turned to pharmaceuticals, who in the end stopped breathing."[8]

Where are we when we are lost, outside of ourselves, on the long road to maybe nowhere? Where are we when we can't breathe anymore, can't see properly, are "outside of ourselves," act desperately, can't tell the difference between violence and love? In fact, classical *Vedanta* philosophy teaches that we are *always* not-lost—that in any moment we can awaken to intimate consciousness—connection with every consciousness, with the universe if you will, with what might be termed "Universal Consciousness"—that connection is what the word "yoga" actually means. Patanjali's Yoga Sutras put it in a slightly more unadorned way: when the fluctuations of the mind cease, union or "yoga" is achieved—then the seer can know the seen in its true nature—then the seer can dwell in the true splendor of his own nature.

There is in yoga practice—metaphysically as well as physically (with the "corpse" posture)—a death of the "self." It's troubling to think that this is the meaning of that word "suicide": "self-killing." Is the taboo and fear of suicide somehow related to the Western anxiety about the true spiritual underpinnings of yoga? In many religions of the world, the suicide victim is literally beyond help: damned for her final act, an act unredeemable.

No one knew her because no one could. It may be significant that Reetika killed herself and her young son, Jehan, in the house of strangers. The two writers who owned the house in which Reetika died have discussed, in an NPR interview in a series on houses, how they exorcised the demons of the house reclaiming the space, replacing the paintings in that room, staying all night in the dining room near the space where Reetika and Jehan died.

Reetika is a ghostly figure in the conversation—neither the host of the program nor ever named by the writers. She's merely referred to as the "houseguest" or "the woman." Her only specific physical presence is when the host asks one of the two what it was like when she found a bar of soap with "one thick black strand of hair" on it. By her actions, she's become dirty—a dark ghost, washing herself with the soap, leaving her hair coiled around it, impolitely haunting the house.

But what if this madness, the fear, the rage—murderous rage or criminal irrationality, it doesn't matter which—is a part of us? What if the demon-poet and ghost-son tagging along can't be exorcised? Can we be safe now that the paintings have been changed and the death has been burned out of the air?

What a sense of betrayal people felt, horror at what happened, yet somehow in this complicated knot of Reetika's and Jehan's deaths, this moment where Reetika, like her father, metaphorically "stopped breathing" and so literally enacted the stopping of her own "breath" has effaced her life, her struggle—her long struggle—to breathe and live, to practice yoga and write poetry. She writes, near the end of "The Art of Breathing," "But I have been given a specific life, the conditions of which are mine to interpret. From suicide to yoga. From fatherlessness to becoming a mother. I have waited so long to have a child, because I have had trouble breathing, trouble owning my skin. There are many things that have aided my release. Poetry. Yoga. I have learned to be grateful for the specifics of my life."[9] T. K. V. Desikachar writes in his book *Heart of Yoga* two seemingly contradictory sentences: "The world exists to be seen and experienced" and "The world exists to set you free." What he means by these sentences is at the heart of the seemingly dualist philosophy of yoga: by fully engaging "the specifics" of a given life, one is given an opportunity to see her or his own "true nature," to become free of attachments—attachments to present conditions, attachments to past preconceptions, attachments to desired outcome—and one can come to dwell in one's own "true splendor."

How can one see one's own true "splendor" other than by living in the world, working through whatever "specifics" are present in any given life? But still so "grateful," yet unable to see one's own "splendor?" It seems like it was a fatal failure of practice, a fatal failure of breathing.

Yet the business of breath is not really so simple. In many times, many places, the breath can catch, even unnoticeably—the body does not receive the oxygen or the *prana* it needs. The inhale or the exhale can become shallow. Learning the "art of breathing" or *pranayama* is supposed to help the individual to take control of the breath; regular practice of it is supposed to heal many ailments, speed the practitioner along on her path to yoga. But that word *pranayama* doesn't actually translate into "art of breathing"—rather it translates as "the restraint of breath." It's by restraint actually that one trains the breathing mechanism and organs to be able to take in full, long, deep, even breaths. Even the root words that make up the Sanskrit word *pranayama* mean "life" and "restraint" (*ayama*, so sonically close to the word for "death," *yama*)—opposites locked tightly up in the practice of breathing. As if at any moment between an inhale and an exhale or between an exhale and an inhale, the other might not follow.

Classical yoga philosophy considers the body to have five "sheaths" beginning with the outermost "physical" sheath and proceeding inward through the sheath of breath, of mind and intellect, until arriving at the innermost sheath, the "bliss" sheath. In the bliss sheath are all the *vasanas*—innermost urges and tendencies that exist deep in the self before they are actualized into the physical world. But if those urges and tendencies are the innermost quality of a human, closest to that human's soul that we are trying to realize the nature of, why is yoga meant to be a surrender of attachment to those very urges? How is it that these deep urges are the same as our true nature when we have been taught all along that our true natures are constant and universal and without urges or tendencies of any kind?

Often times when I am on the yoga mat in a posture, the teacher will give instructions that take my body in different directions. They seem contradictory instructions—"twist further to the right while you take your left sitting bone straight down to the mat"—but actually they complement the stretch within the body. The spine stretches slowly, lovingly, without rush, over the course of months and years (or, depending on what you believe, over lifetimes) and not over seconds of a single stretch or across ninety minutes of a single class.

How can I deny that *vasana* of rage or insanity embedded in my own experience? A woman who practiced my same practices of yoga and poetry was led not only to bliss and union, but also in the end to desperate action, to murder and self-death, not of the bliss induced yogic variety, but actual ending. This is not reassuring.

Yoga will not save me. Poetry will not save me. The act of breathing can get caught up in knots in a dozen different ways. So why should we be "saved"? *Vedanta* teaches that life is *maya*—an illusion—a nonapprehension of the Reality; yet at the same time, this "nonapprehension" of Reality is considered to be inexplicably inherently part of the same supreme Reality. Meanwhile Lalla and the Kashmiri Shaivites began interpreting the same concept but in another way: it is not that the universe is *maya* but that every part of it is a manifestation of Universal Consciousness.

At the heart of my practice of writing poems is the idea that each poem attempts to launch from unknown to unknown. Each poem carries with it my double-prayer: that it carry some of that truth, that it be an honest and musical messenger, and also that it not—that some of that mystery be incommunicable, so the writing and reading of poems can continue. This same dichotomy lies at the heart of yoga practice: a practice toward union with some kind of Consciousness, at the heart of which is *maya,* or nonapprehension of that same Consciousness. "Stillness" is not the endless holding of breath, nor an endless inhale, nor an endless exhale, but a constant cycle. There is life and death and then there are the silent spaces, places in our breath, where for some of us only our poetry and our yoga can take us.

There was a sculpture in the middle of the forest trails near my home in the mid-Hudson valley. It's a big boulder built of a single edition of the *Poughkeepsie Journal,* put together by a high school science class years ago to study how paper decomposes. The citizens were up in arms at the ugliness of it. Each season passes and the boulder sheds its paper flecks into the water, the air, gets damper, gets moldier. This morning as we walked by it in the winter-turning it seemed green and brown, finally coming to resemble part of the landscape. All things are part of breath. All things return. In *World Hotel* the fictional mother tells her daughter, "*I am proud to have borne you/When you gather around me/ newness comes into the world.*"[10]

At one time in her life, Reetika was grateful for the "specifics" of her life, the joy of her son, her yoga and her poetry. She wrote at the end of the poem "From Patanjali," which appeared at the end of her essay: "you/son deep sleep dreamless/my own skin I am in/you in your rest and/above everything I wish you well."[11] If in yoga reality and nonapprehension lie in each other's arms, then our greatest "flaws" are actually our truest nature, perhaps somewhere all the lost and failed and wandering are yet home. In the breath.

In the continuation of breath one finds always eternal life in the present moment.

I've stopped wondering what my yoga practice, my breathing will do for me. Will it make me stronger? Take me to that bliss room? Will I be able to write the poem-boats to sail aloft on the breath of the music in my body? I know the postures are the boat—breath is the wind. All the sadnesses and angers are still with me, all the betrayals and losses still with me, all crewing my journey. May the water too be "still": because only by taking these strange partners, the ghost poet and her child as well, into my breath, can I breathe fully, truly, can my practice be complete.

Breathe. Be "still."

Notes

1. Vazirani, "The Art of Breathing," 64–65.
2. Barks, 58.
3. Vazirani, "The Art of Breathing," 63.
4. Vazirani, 68.
5. Vazirani, *World Hotel*, 65.
6. Vazirani, "The Art of Breathing, 74.
7. Span.
8. Vazirani, 74.
9. Vazirani, 74.
10. Vazirani, *World Hotel*, 69.
11. Vazirani, *Radha Says*, 39.

Part 2

What's American about
American Poetry?

On the tenth anniversary of their symposium "What's American about American Poetry?"—which I had attended as a younger man—I was invited by the Poetry Society of America, along with several other poets, to reflect again on this question. It never occurred to me to write about anything other than writers from Indigenous American communities—their poetry and poetics seeming to me to be the closest literal answer to the question.

I wondered what was meant in the first place by the term "American." It neither really defines national origin, geographical placement ("America" outsourcing itself far beyond its own continental borders to islands across the world) nor linguistic or cultural unity. This country resists itself, has always resisted itself; what it claims to be chafes always against its reality. One of the reasons for this, of course, is that in its founding it delineated a set of defining values for itself that were false; those of different colored skin and different genders were excluded from the polity. More than two centuries in and we are still defined by gender- and heterosexist-based inequality enforced by executive, legislative and judicial law. This disconnect between thought and deed is part of what must be thought of as "American."

"American" must also mean multiplicities as we are a nation of countless ethnicities, countless languages and countless experiences, none of which have a greater or lesser claim to life in the "nation" than any other. And truth be told, in a place where any place has two names or more, we are not "one nation" after all, but many. When we think of a unified or singular American identity, we lose the chance to truly understand our selves and one another. As Bryan Bearhart writes:[1]

Biitan-akiing-enabijig is Ojibwe.
I can't tell you what it means.
    We sit on cuspis.
    A horizon. A margin.
    What makes us "not them."
I only wish I could speak in tongue.

Bearhart makes a breathless grammatical mistake in the last line here, dreaming himself to a monolingual expression he knows he can never nor will ever have. A postmodern aesthetic shows us, on the other hand, the rich possibilities of living in the in-between zones, the horizons, the margins—our chance is to become a pluralistic society, diminishing old class, gender, race, national and sexual lines that configured most historically hierarchical world societies, and then reconfigure a new "American" society that functions on collective enterprise, cultural and artistic growth, and individual human development and betterment.

The "American Dream" has always been not communitarian but individual, based on not only a desire but a need to "get ahead," despite any shortcomings. So, to cite only one example, Malcolm X once criticized our Civil Rights Movement for orienting itself around the individual right to vote or participate in unsegregated arenas of commerce (buses, businesses, restaurants), rather than building class-based solidarity within the United States with labor unions and movements and international solidarity with African nations who were at the same time struggling for independence against European and American powers, who controlled mineral interests and thus the political and economic institutions of power on the continent. As Malcolm pointed out, without diamonds for industrial machines, all modern progress would (literally) grind to a halt. These were the types of connections between political theories and organizing communities that both he and, several years later, Martin Luther King Jr. were beginning to build when each was killed.

Is another part of being "American" this self-orientation toward our own concerns and what happens within our own borders, while still requiring the labor, water, land and mineral resources of every other place in the world? In other words, our material comfort, cultural production and individual human development and betterment does not rely on any reconfigurement of gender-, race-, class-, or nation-based hierarchies, but actually on an institution of them backed up by American military power (easy when more than 50 cents of every tax dollar goes to support that power), and global political and financial institutions.

We are a long way from the hoped-for definition of "American" we aspire to and still aspire to somewhere in our minds, I believe. So as "American" poets, we do have both versions of America within us, since as citizens of the polity we still do (mostly) benefit from our luck and our willingness to go along, by continuing to elect and support leaders who subscribe to the "American Exceptionalism" doctrine and use U.S. financial and military power to support it.

But we have a chance also, with our language, with the form and focus of our art to begin delineating the truth of our lives as it is and to start imagining on paper and in space the differences we hope to enact.

In Sherwin Bitsui's *Flood Song* he writes of a lost connection among language, locality and lived experience. In speaking of his grandfather, he writes:[2]

Years before, he would have named this season

By flattening a field where grasshoppers jumped into
black smoke.

The season, in this case, like the American landscape itself, is not named for the explorer's imperialist ambitions—as Paul Virilio once claimed, the American imperial object is ever outward: once the Pacific was reached, the incursions continued into the ocean itself; once the hands of empire reached out and around the planet and met each other coming, the direction changed into outer space—or for a romantic idea of the self defined from or manipulated by "nature" rather than the psychic and kinetic qualities of the land itself.

When the Poetry Society of America convened a number of poets—Sonia Sanchez, Michael Palmer, Louise Glück, Jorie Graham, Kimiko Hahn and many others—to discuss the question

"What's American About American Poetry?" a general consensus tentatively, if affably, emerged—a single lively panel kerfuffle between Thylias Moss and John Hollander aside—that the most "American" quality was the quality of constant undefinability. Was it a cop-out?

If the strength of American poetry is its hybrid qualities and leanings, its weakness is also particularly American: its amnesia of history and language, but not a passive amnesia of forgetting, rather a brutal and intentional act of erasure: towns and neighborhoods named after plants, animals and people who no longer exist there. There is a city in Florida called Miami and, more than a thousand miles away in Ohio, there is a river called Miami. You have to draw a line that stretches the distance all between those two places to spell out even the first letter of the word "America." And where are the Miami now? That's the start of the second letter.

In M. L. Smoker's poem "From the River's Edge," she writes about the fragmentation inherent in being separated from one's sources by a larger external narrative and the ability of poetry to bridge that divide: "Can a poet speak of a/second version of her mother?" She goes on to write:[3]

> The one who lives in a
> silent cave where she allows no visitors, gives no interviews.
> Her memoir is being written there by a shadow seven feet
> tall that can hold no pen or pencil, both hands missing.
> My living mother dreams of new waters that have no
> adequate translation.

So in this historical moment, the possibilities of the various American languages seem twofold: either to homogenize and smooth out all difference (one American urge) or to continue to splinter, refract one another, create dozens of new and glorious forms of creative expression.

And about nations and languages that have disappeared or been suppressed: history isn't just something that happened. As Utah Phillips said, "The past didn't go anywhere." Native, indigenous and aboriginal populations on the American continent and around the world struggle every day for political self-determination and ownership of their own local land and mineral resources; in other words liberation from imperialism, whether political, economic or cultural.

So what we really need, every American poet, are forms and approaches and languages like Sherwin Bitsui's, M. L. Smoker's, Bryan Bearhart's, and, for example, Dawn Lundy Martin's, Gillian Conoley's, Mark Nowak's, Myung Mi Kim's, C. D. Wright's; forms that hold within them the voices of alterity, the parallels of experience, are lyric and narrative forms that embrace and present new possibilities of understanding America and American experiences.

At the end of his poem "Ars Poetica," Orlando White writes beautifully of the real physical and erotic possibilities when language and experience twist around each other, when the form of the lyric is allowed to fracture and grow anew under the pressure of contemporary realities of alienation, distance and technology:[4]

I opened an envelope addressed to me. I pulled out a blank
    sheet of paper, unfolded it.

In the letter: no message, no sender's name, just a white
    space.

"I like that you exist," she said. Like the lowercase i, my body
    felt present on a
page: fitted in a dark suit, white necktie, and inside the black
    dot, a smile.

But it was the way her skin felt as she dressed into a black
    outfit. The way her
body slipped into a long dark dress shaped like a shadow.

He picked up a stone; held it to his ear. Shook it like a
    broken watch. He opened
it, and inside were small gears, shaped like a clock.

I am a skeleton, a sentence, too. Although like you, I am
    neither a meaning nor
a structure, just silence in a complete thought.

111

Here language itself lives, changes through our actions. The stone has little gears inside and why wouldn't it: it is telling time. "In the Lakota language," Layli Long Soldier wrote to me, "the word for God or Creator, which is 'Tunkasila' which also means grandfather . . . But the root of Tunkasila is 'Tunkan'—which means stone, a sacred stone or a stone of great power. What is the connection between a stone and God/grandfather?" In White's case, who is Diné rather than Lakota, it seems not only the stones that speak but every component of conceptual and physical meaning-making.

Besides supporting art like this, art that confronts all dimensions of the "American" experience, we have to acknowledge also the real military, political and economic empire as well as the cultural apparatus, what Nowak calls the "Neo-Liberal Language Industry" in his excellent short book *Workers of the Word, Unite and Fight!*—that supports that matrix of reality: a reality in which notions of "plurality" and "hybridity" and "alterity" are just three more convenient ways of organizing a population into compliant behavior and tokenizing a couple of voices in order to avoid seeing or seeking out the rest of them.

After all, our present machine-driven sense of geographical placelessness isn't real. History and geography *so* still play a role in daily life in America. Jean Baudrillard in his book *America* painted a stark picture of our current landscape as a vacant series of sites of consumption (strip malls, some of which are even *designed* to imitate the small-town America main streets they brutally replaced), housing developments and parking lots linked by an interstate system, but it isn't really true. The urban spaces and wildlife, under duress and real political attack (especially by defunding public schools and university systems), still struggle to actualize their possible roles as instruments for a revitalization of real and substantial creative and cultural life.

Our multilingualism and cultural openness have made many spaces in poetry. Kimiko Hahn's writing between poetry and prose, Meena Alexander's innovations in the lyric between sense and sound (especially in her latest book *Quickly Changing River*), Agha Shahid Ali's transportation (literally) of the ghazal into English (or was it that he transported English-language poetry to the form of the ghazal?) are all examples that seem particularly American to me, as much the benefit of English as a meeting place.

Indian English, I can tell you, is a separate language, both spoken and written, from American English. It has different words, different intonations and pronunciations, different accepted sentence order, different syntax. In my book *Bright Felon* I tried as hard as I could to tell the story of my life the only way I knew how. I did not have the intention of writing "poetry" or "poems" or "memoir" while I was doing it, only sentences. The genre-queerness of that book, called both poetry and prose and prose-poetry, is specifically related to the idea that life-writing should follow the patterns of a "by-the-book" formula of chapter, structure, sentence and paragraph, that a life can't fundamentally be "queer," impossible to tell in any other way. And besides, I'm not the first one to try it: Etel Adnan, Mahmoud Darwish, Alistair McCartney, Sarah Manguso and so many others I am sure have written prose memoirs that dispense with all the usual expectations of what the form ought to do.

Writers like Myung Mi Kim or Sherwin Bitsui or Tracie Morris are actually making new spaces in American poetry, both in terms of what poetry is supposed to look and sound like and also in terms of what its social function as literature actually is. Lucille Clifton wrote, "i was born in babylon/ both nonwhite and woman./ i had no models."[5] At least in terms of poetry, for myself, I no longer feel this way: I feel there are so many models for me now.

We have a timeless tradition to draw from. At the original "What's American About American Poetry" symposium in 1999, John Hollander caused a little bit of controversy when he criticized Thylias Moss for citing "the landscape" as her literary forebear. The two had a somewhat testy exchange that ended when Moss leapt up onto her chair and declared to the room, "Some of us don't have people as literary forebears. For some of us whose ancestors lay in holds of slaveships, a crack of blue seen between the planes of wood was our literary forebear."

In dg nanouk okpik's poem cycle "For-the-spirits-who-have-rounded-the-bend," she confronts the tradition of the "identity" and "coming-of-age" poems in surprising and inventive ways that marry a concern with sound to the more traditional folk images.

113

Rather than being a marrying of opposites, in okpik's work, it feels absolutely contemporary and unified:[6]

> . . . Then as the ligature of Inuit light flux and flows
> like herds of walrus, passing along the coast, Yes then, but
> maybe
> this is a seal hook of bear claws clipping me to the northern
> tilt,
> pinning me to the cycle of night when the day slows, the
> wind
> shifts to cloud, and the moon shadow grows to sun loops.

Since she is clipped to the "northern tilt" and pinned to movements of night and day, she is able to discover through the process of transformation she undergoes throughout the poem that nothing is lost, that she can live wholly and fully, connected to all her various human and animal sources. There is a danger in it, to be sure, but in the end it is the winged heart that speaks of hope and strength:[7]

> . . . After the border of flesh and church, after the old book
> is read,
> and ivory with scrimshaw is used with rib tools to create
> Okvik
> not Christianity, when the bell tones across the sound, until
> then,
> I will wash ashore in a dazed white-out, hide flesh to beach
> with my fore-claws hanging limply, my hooded golden
> eyes with concentric circles, lines on my chin,
> with a large backbone for my lungs, and a heart of spotted
> wings.

I think of something Naomi Shihab Nye wrote, in 1999, in her response to the question "What's American About American Poetry?" Nye said, "When I was working overseas on various occasions, poets in other countries would remark that we American poets have a luxury they do not have: we are free to write about tiny 'insignificances' any time we want to . . . We write about personal lives, minor idiosyncrasies, familial details, tomatoes—not feeling burdened to explore larger collective issues all the time, which is something writers elsewhere often consider part of their endless responsibility."[8]

There is a way in which all American life, American writing and poetry included, participates in the historical (and geographical!) amnesia inherent in the concept of "America." What is the responsibility of the writer? When you look one place, there is another place you are not looking. We will have to think for a long time to figure out where we are and who we are and what we are doing in this place, thought to be ours from "sea to shining sea," ours by some form of "manifest destiny," some form of "American exceptionalism."

In her essay "Poetics of Generosity," Judith E. Johnson writes, "I am not Alterity: I will not play that role in your mind or in my own. I am not Shakespeare's sister Judith, whose existence Virginia Woolf divined in her prophetic sanity. I am Judith, and Shakespeare is this Judith's brother." She refuses to be defined by her "absence from the center of discourse." She goes on to suggest a new way of thinking about the American poetic land-scape:[9]

> Jane Austen, the Brontë sisters, and George Eliot define the 19th
> Century English novel; if that definition does not hold Dickens,
> Thackeray, and Meredith, they are the deviation from the norm,
> and their Alterity makes them contingent. Ethel Schwabacher
> defines Abstract Expressionism; Jackson Pollack is the deviation.
> Muriel Rukeyser defines the poetics of energy-transfer; Charles
> Olson is the deviation . . . you, our illustrious male colleagues and
> brothers, are the deviation. It will be healthy for you to see
> yourselves in the full brilliance of your own Alterity for a while,
> to study our practice as the human norm, and to wonder when
> and why you strayed from us.

American poets have so much to learn from each other; it has always been precisely those underseen or underheard texts that have provided the greatest influence on the literary landscape at large when they are revealed. Need we any more proof than Dickinson's poems, Nin's uncensored diaries, Melville's late stories? In the case of all three, gender and sexuality were at play in the suppression. Recent attention paid to a younger crop of indigenous writers—a recent weekend of events at Poets House, a feature on Native women writers that Long Soldier edited for *Drunken Boat,* Long Soldier herself being featured by the Academy of American Poets in their magazine, Orlando White being selected for Poetry Society of America's "New American Poets" festival (by me, I will admit), Natalie Diaz winning an American Book Award for her first collection—points to a long hoped for shift in attitudes toward Indigenous writing, not as "contingent" but as the *real* mainstream of "American literary tradition."

Natalie Diaz is one of the most exciting poets I have read recently. In her poem "Soirée Fantastique," she takes ancient European myth and weaves it together with contemporary American situations and idiom:[10]

> Houdini arrived first, with Antigone on his arm.
> Someone should have told her it was rude
> to chase my brother in circles with such a shiny shovel.
> She only said, I'm building the man a funeral.
> But last I measured, my brother was still a boy.

As with most wild parties featuring the dead, things can only get crazier when Jesus shows up:

> There are violins playing. The violins are on fire—
> they are passed around until we're all smoking. Jesus coughs,
> climbs down from the cross of railroad ties above the table.
> He's a regular at these carrion revelries, and it's annoying
> how he turns the bread to fish, especially when we have
>   sandwiches.

Neither the escape artist, nor the son of god, two men who specialized in fulfilling destinies, are able to console Antigone and explain to her why she will not be permitted to bury the young brother. Only the speaker of the poem is left to explain it to her, taking away her spade, saying:

> We aren't here to eat, we are being eaten.
> Come, pretty girl. Let us devour our lives.

Part of our answer is to now start experiencing poetry not solely in the mind, nor solely visually, nor solely aurally but through all the senses at once. When I commented to Layli Long Soldier that I felt something of the influence of Gertrude Stein in her poems, she told me of her appreciation of Stein by both sight and sound, and of her various other influences including Cubist painters and Canadian writer bpNichol. Referencing Stein, she told me of the traditional "jingle-dress" in many Native American cultures, a dress which would literally create a sonic experience as the wearer moved around in space. Here is the beginning of Long Soldier's prose poem "Edge":[11]

> This drive along the road the bend the banks behind the
>   wheel
> I am called Mommy. My name is Mommy on these drives the
> sand and brush the end of winter we pass. You in the
>   rearview
> double buckled back center my love. Your mother's mouth
>   has
> a roof your mother's mouth is a church. A hut in a field lone
> standing. The thatched roof has caught spark what flew from
> walls the spark apart from rock from stable meaning.

It's not enough to say as Americans we have to understand our history. We have to also understand the here and now, the voices we have not heard, couldn't or wouldn't, voices that help to construct and reveal new rooms in the houses of our understanding.

Stein said the wildest thing—I still love it—about America: "America is now the oldest country in the world because by the methods of the civil war and the commercial conceptions that followed it America created the twentieth century." We can talk for a long time about what she meant, but the most interesting part for me is how America has gone—militarily, economically, culturally—global. The way I think about it, Mahmoud Darwish is a most "American" poet. He and his family fled his home in Palestine in 1947; returning without papers, he lived in internal exile for most of his young life, and then as an expatriate in Moscow, Tripoli, Beirut and Paris, before finally returning home in 1997. His poetry constantly engaged with the question of "exile," but it wasn't long before he realized that "exile" is a spiritual and metaphysical condition as well. How much more "American," or true to the American experience, both indigenous and immigrant, can you get?

He came to America only once, for an operation on his heart. Fady Joudah, the Palestinian-American poet who has been translating Darwish, writes a beautiful essay about his first and only meeting with Darwish—at a coffee shop in the local supermall. In that peculiarly American locale, poet and translator talk together for the first time, sharing stories, talking about poetry.

And that's the key, isn't it? In this life, supported by millions of gallons of oil, this strange life of buildings dropped on top of scoured land, this weird American landscape, this odd reality in which our primary responsibility as flesh and bone entities seems to be to consume, to receive and spend money, well where do you find the poetry, by which I mean any spiritual sustenance at all?

At any rate, I think the "American Century" is soon over. Within the next thirty or forty years, when the global food production and distribution system, utterly unsustainable, moves into crisis, when water availability and sustainability move into a crisis point, as fossil fuels begin to evaporate and disappear, only societies who have been able to do more with less will be able to cope. Our society will necessarily be required to start making real and concrete steps in this direction, exploring free energy, free health care and free primary, secondary and higher education for everyone within the borders.

Sometime in the next century, we will have to learn, probably quickly and in an atmosphere of duress (whether external or internal or some combination of the two), how to live without many of the things we take very much for granted—to cite three varied examples: fresh vegetables in the winter, regularly scheduled air travel and round-the-clock availability of electrical power and tap-water. Are we heading back to pioneer days? We will be pioneering in our own hearts the routes of connected-ness between us and the earth, us and everyone around us.

Language, modes of communication and availability of communication media will be critically important in the new world; they will save us, and by us I mean *all* of us: one of the things I think will need to happen is an end to Nationalism, not an end to nations, necessarily, but an end to the project of nation-building certainly. We will necessarily return to locally based economies and with it, naturally, we will probably return to locally based languages and forms of cultural expressions and a form of multilingualism quite common in the world and in marginal American populations but not yet in the mainstream.

As access to fresh water diminishes, silicon production must necessarily dwindle, so I wonder what the future of electronics will be. We'll find a way to stay in touch with each other, I'm sure of that, but I think a return to the most ancient sources of art, dance and poetry seems also inevitable. I think poetry will move back to the oral, back to the musical and back to the mysterious and spiritual and difficult.

Long Soldier's poem "Edge" continues:

Large car steady at the curve palest light driest day a field
of rocks we are not poor sealed in windows. You hum in the
    back.
I do not know what to say how far to go the winter near dead
as we drive you do not understand word for word the word
for you is little. But you hear how it feels always. The music
plays you swing your feet. And I see it I Mommy the edge
but do not point do not say look as we pass the heads gold
and blowing these dry grasses eaten in fear by man and
    horses.

It draws both from her own personal experiences, landscape and physical environment, the sound textures of Stein, and a postmodern linguistic and theoretical sensibility. With visionary work like this, which looks backward and forward at once, which encompasses all of the magnificent differences and all the "Americas."

Maybe it is better for us to look at work like this—Bitsui, White, Long Soldier, Diaz, Bearhart, okpik—as the real American poetry, and what we think of as the Anglo-American literary tradition as the tradition of alterity, of deviation, that this landscape, on this continent, this strange life, needs to be explained in terms of contemporary Native writers who have been able to fuse the Anglo-American literary tradition with Native languages, poetics and forms of expression.

As for me, let me wander anywhere and hope Darwish is waiting for me. True, he is buried in Palestine, but he died here, in a hospital in Texas, and perhaps something of his spirit also lingers here, haunting the place, reminding us, as he wrote in his great poem "Speech of the Red Indian":[12]

> Oh white man, of all the dead who are still dying, both those
>   who live and those who return to tell the tale
>
> Let's give the earth enough time to tell the whole truth
> about you and us.
>
> The whole truth about us.
>
> The whole truth about you.

Notes

1. Bearhart, 9.
2. Bitsui, 6.
3. Smoker, 17.
4. White, 54.
5. Clifton, 427.
6. okpik, 70.
7. okpik, 74.
8. Nye.
9. Johnson, manuscript given to Kazim Ali.
10. Diaz, 66.
11. Long Soldier.
12. Darwish, *The Adam of Two Edens*, 147.

Poet Crossing Borders

1.

He is looking into my book, turning each page slowly, looking at it closely as if he was reading, perusing the faded blue marks there. Every once in a while he touches his fingertip to the page, leaves it there before slowly turning it.

"What is it?" I ask, knowing what he sees there. He does not answer. "My name is Mohammad Kazim Ali. I am a college professor. You can call up the school's webpage and see my profile there." He does not answer. "I am a *poet*," I say.

It is the spring of 2006. It is still a year before a student at the Pennsylvania university I then taught at will see me in the parking lot outside my office in the English Department, carrying a box of recycling to the curb. He will call the police to report suspicious activity. The campus will be temporarily shut down. In the rush to fulfill all the emergency procedures they will forget to notify the department secretary still inside the building at her desk. At some point in the afternoon she will look out the window and see the bomb squad and panic. I am not aware of this. I am in my little love-bug, driving north to Carlisle, humming along with the radio. Maybe poetry *is* dangerous?

"OK," says the passport control officer, shutting my book and knocking its edge against the counter between us. "You need to go with this man," he says and hands the passport to another officer waiting.

Because the second officer, the one that will take me into the back room and to my habitual indignity, is also Asian, a Filipino, I get bold. "Do we really need to do this?" I ask him. "You realize I have to go through this *every* time."

He does not answer.

I heft my shoulder bag. He does a quick double-take when he catches a glance of my fingernails, painted in what I think is a fetching slate blue. He keeps walking. I am annoyed immediately but what is more disturbing—that he doesn't immediately understand that I would pose no Al-Qaeda-supported security threat, or is it worse—that somehow I take this sign of my Westernization and postmodernity to be a marker of queerness and thus excusing me from scrutiny, an evasion that perhaps any other Muslim man with more heteronormative behavior would not be able to escape? That somehow I am trying, from a position of odd privilege, to be clear that I am not "that kind of Muslim," that I am not *like them.*

When the truth is that any Muslim body is strange now, other, worthy of scrutiny.

And to cross any border at all means to submit one's own body to the law.

The law marks the body, documents it, scrutinizes it, registers it, permits it, manipulates it, suppresses it, denies it, forbids it, kills it.

To be a nationalist means to believe in a "nation." Linguistically it may mean your "natal" place—where you were born—but within that conception is an intrinsic connection (of political loyalty yes but also physically in the tissues and organs themselves) of a human body to the geographic location or space in which it entered the world or currently resides.

To be "international" must mean then to be "between" nations, between loyalties, between the human body and the very idea of a law that seeks to control it. It must be a good place for a poet to be, a person who speaks with a forked tongue who understands the difference between sky and *caelo* may be just a little drifting but that between *sky* and *ciel* is immeasurable distance, not mere vowel and consonant.

At Babel we were given fractured tongues and the notions of multiplicity and infinity opened themselves in our mouths. Say something. Say something more.

It is not when I cross a border but when I cross *back*—back to my own home, my "nation," as it were—that my body is subjected to various technological interventions. I am separated from the group. X-rays pass through me. An image of me, a naked ghost, appears somewhere then disappears. I disappear. Led by a man—usually younger, usually a man of color, usually either he or I are joking to hide our discomfort—to the cordoned-off room. Here we are: me, shoeless and trembling, trying to ignore his uniform and gun, his hands moving up and down my body. He is giving me—it must be part of the training—a running narration of his activity.

I am touching your chest. I am touching your stomach now. I am going to touch your groin. I will only use the back of my hand. I am touching the inside of your thigh. Your hip.

My body is the dark one. My name is a Muslim one. Your name is in our system. We know it isn't you. You should change your name. What is your father's name. What is your grandfather's name. Who are you. Where do you come from. We know it isn't you but your name is in our system.

Body you do me well and dangerous, slip between nations, between tongues, slip yourself naked between night and day between genders and genres.

Or will you write yourself in code, download your short-term memory into machines, slide credit cards under the skin of your palm, be tagged by an electronic surveillance device. Will your physical location be monitored like the airplane on the screen slowly crawling across the Midwest to New York, crawling from New York to Iceland, from Iceland across Europe and Turkey to Tel Aviv.

What is your father's name. What is your grandfather's name. Wrote Darwish, "My homeland is not a suitcase." My suitcase is opened, all my things taken out, rubbed with special cloth. The cloth is taken away to be tested. For what I don't know.

This is how a poet crosses borders.

2.

I was driven from the sea through the mountains to Jerusalem. Where every street has three names that do not always translate from one to another. Street of the "Mujahideen," meaning "martyrs," is translated into English and Hebrew as "Lion's Gate Road." But the "mujahideen" are not the twentieth-century martyrs but instead refer to the men who fought with Saladdin nearly a thousand years earlier.

History has long arms in a country crossed and recrossed by lines. Buildings, neighborhoods and whole cities are built one on top of another. Of course the first thing I wanted to see in Jerusalem was Al-Aqsa, called by Muslims "the Far Mosque," called by Jewish people the Temple Mount. As we climbed the creaky wooden causeway for non-Muslim worshipers, we could see through the slat-walls Jewish worshipers who had come to the small remaining fragment of the Western Wall. It was an emotional sight: a people wandering still in the only land they call home, still hovering at a remnant and in very temporary settings—sitting in plastic lawn chairs or dragging makeshift podiums over on which to place their prayer books.

Perhaps the temporariness of the furnishings is meant to acknowledge the fleeting nature of the ruin, or perhaps it is a form of resistance—that to have more permanent accoutrements would be to accept that the Temple was lost and would never be reclaimed. And there, just ahead of us on the causeway, the other side of the whole equation—twenty or thirty body-length riot-shields, stacked with easy reach for quick use. Then I remember how places—all places—are used as symbols of the "nation," how Ground Zero is used, how this place is used too for swearing-in ceremonies for elite units of the Israeli army.

On the Mount itself one finds the enormous Dome of the Rock and a mosque, built and destroyed many times. Around the mosque in the great tree-lined park, many small groups of men reciting the Quran. As with many Muslim mosques, it is not the building but the space itself that is important. In this case, the rock under the mosque. When you go inside there is a little stairwell under the rock that leads into the so-called well of souls. Where one can and can't pray is fraught here with all kinds of meaning. When a group of Jewish men came up onto the plaza the Muslim men began reciting loudly pronouncing the words as if declaiming to a large audience, merely sonic resistance perhaps but a resistance nonetheless. One of the Arab men called the Jewish people "settlers," which I didn't at first understand.

I had always thought of settlers as people out in the territories building their kibbutzim but soon I learned that it isn't so. There are settlers inside Palestinian cities like Hebron and there are even settlers buying up or confiscating Palestinian buildings and apartments inside the Muslim Quarter of the old city and in East Jerusalem. You know them by the enormous Israeli flags hanging from the roof and by the barbed wire, surveillance cameras and other security measures. Normally, Israeli citizens are forbidden by rabbinical law to step foot on the Temple Mount. Those two generally come as a provocation. Hence the shouted prayers, the only response the Muslim men can offer to assert their own right to the space.

I cross the border—the fake border, the invisible one, the so-called Green Line because it was drawn on a map with a green crayon—between Jerusalem and Ramallah by calling a cab. Though others with less money who catch the six-shekel bus are required to dismount and walk through the checkpoint in four stages by advancing through metal cages, I pay my cab driver two hundred shekels and am driven straight through. Because he has an Israeli license plate I am driven on the Israeli roads. I arrive in Ramallah in under twenty minutes. The journey through the checkpoint takes ninety minutes or more.

As far as borders go, this one has got high drama—border patrols, metal detectors, full searches, plus a thirty-foot high concrete wall wrapped in barbed wire and mounted by observation posts. The soldiers aren't much more than children but I think children grow up quickly in this country. On the Israeli side the bare concrete is licked here and there by the odd piece of liberation graffiti—"Occupiers Out!" "Free Palestine!"—and on the Palestinian side it is covered with a rich tapestry of art: twenty-foot-tall portraits of Yasser Arafat and Marwan Barghouti, drawings of birds, flowers, animals, a Banksy drawing of a young girl holding balloons being borne up and over the wall.

It is not a wall in every place. For long stretches of countryside it is "nothing more" than a high chain-link fence with layers of barbed wire. An electrified fence.

3.

If you want to think about how the machinery of "nations" works against the individual human body there is no better body to start with than the Palestinian body, specifically the body of Mahmoud Darwish, on August 6, 1982, on his hands and knees, crawling down the hallway of his third-floor Beirut apartment while bombs hit the upper floors of the same building, crawling down the hallway to the kitchen so he can make a pot of coffee.

Coffee during bombs: "I want nothing more from the passing days than the aroma of coffee," he says. "The aroma of coffee so I can hold myself together, stand on my feet, and be transformed from something that crawls into a human being."[1] It is in the midst of war or occupation that people reach for the smallest thing, like Darwish's coffee—"the virgin of the silent morning," "the sister of time,"—that gives their body's experience back to itself.

Occupied by the time of war and invasions, the natural places in the world—not only its mountains and forests but also its cities and towns and human settlements—give up their identities to steel and fire. Darwish writes of the sparkling Mediterranean: "The sea has been entirely packed into stray shells. It is changing its marine nature and turning into metal. Does death have all these names?"[2]

In myths of creation it is given to humans to name things in the world, that is, to give all the particularities of the world their significances. When we tried to climb back into formlessness, namelessness—God?—the tower fell and we were punished—rewarded?—by the splintering of tongues, the *Babel*.

When I went to France I went without language. I lived nearly mute as the soft, sanded-off edges of French disappeared into my ears without cognizance. It took *reading* for me to finally learn the words and be able to speak. It took *writing* for me to at last be able to make sentences. I lived alone on Corsica, having an easier time understanding Corsican French, French with an Italian accent if you will.

Even so I could only write in English what I knew in French and the translation wasn't by meaning but by sound. "I am sending you the sands of Corsica," I wrote on a postcard. And under it led by the assonance between verb and object I left the sand as itself—*sable*—but found a new verb to match sound of it, "*j'oublie les sables de la Corse . . .*"

So I slipped between tongues. Urdu and Arabic, since I was young, had always been in my ear, and Arabic had been in my mouth too, but French was the first other tongue that traveled among them. My muscles—my tongue, the shape of my mouth and lips, the constriction of my throat—all had to change to accommodate it. But they—my throat in particular—had had good practice from Arabic. And sound does give you meaning. *La mer sans cesse,* I whispered to myself on a blustery November morning walking along the Oregon coast. I could not translate it. Will you do it for me. I am forgetting the sands of Corsica.

So untranslated my genre: essays called poems, poems called novels, and some things that call themselves nothing, call themselves wind. A novel, a notebook, a score. Score, not that you won something but that you marked something down on the stone or the wall, a mark to remind you that utterance follows no genre, the body is gendered in order to control it, to promote the continuity of ownership of resources through and past the individual body's decay and death. Such continuity of ownership—call it inheritance, call it shareholding, call it capital—is required to have prosperity at all—prosperity for the few requires the labor of many.

So what is a body for? To utter or to work. And work for whom. Questions of language, nation and individual human body—its fears, its lusts, its sweetness and kindness—are not unrelated.

Darwish knows he is in trouble when the birds stop singing. "Perhaps one of the worst Arabic words is *ta:'irah*—airplane—which is the feminine form of *ta:'ir*—bird . . . Two wings of steel and silver versus two made of feathers. A nose of wiring and steel against a beak made of song. A cargo of rockets against a grain of wheat and straw. Their skies no longer safe, the birds stop singing and pay heed to the war."[3]

4.

Perhaps inspired by the tent city protests across Israel during the summer of 2011 or perhaps then again not, hundreds of protesters took to Wall Street in New York City in the fall of that year. They are, as I write this word, out there still. Those of us not close think about logistics—the twisting narrow streets of the financial district of Manhattan lend themselves better perhaps to a real "occupation" than the wide and windy four-lane grid streets of downtown Cleveland. Can you have the political momentum, in other words, without the physical action. On-line activism seems to take you only so far.

Suddenly, the imagination is captured—a whole coalition assembles itself not around the *idea* at all but around the actual physical bodies, the cold ones, the beaten ones, the tear-gassed ones, that are in the park on Wall Street or crossing the Brooklyn Bridge and entering the prison system. Like Indians marching on the salt mills in colonial India, the aim seems to be a pure volume of bodies, undeniable in their physical presence.

One of the questions the Wall Street protests make us ask is: where are the roots of Western financial power? And their routes—where do they lead us next? Malcolm X pointed out that the colonization of Africa, perhaps fueled by racist ideology, happened because of the economic and mineral needs of the developed West. In particular, he pointed out, for cobalt, nickel and diamonds. Not ornamental diamonds, he scolded, but industrial diamonds, without which all the military power of the West would grind to a halt. So today we add oil. The map looks different but the intent is the same.

When Donna Haraway asks "Why should our bodies end at the skin, or include at best other beings encapsulated by skin?"[4] she means to explain the idea that our environment—the natural and the made objects within it—are an expression both inward and outward of our individual, communal, bodily and national desires. So these extensions—the things that make us "cyborgs," or compromise our biological distinctiveness—can in reverse-direction instead tell us who we really are.

Technologies that intervene in the Palestinian body: airplanes, bombs hitting the apartment building, guns in the hands of soldiers of various factions, the sea covered in metal, the sky a helmet of steel, surveillance equipment, cameras that photograph the body, scanners that read code on ID cards and passports, systems that take measure of the body's shape, bullets that enter it. That was the real punchline behind what the Israeli youth were calling the "Israeli Summer"—that no one was willing to draw the connection between the economic downturn gripping Israel and nearly fifty years of military-industrial-complex–driven occupation of the West Bank and the Strip. Far from being required for "security," the Israeli occupation of 1967 is just good—very very good—business.

And Darwish? Still in the kitchen, painstakingly describing the making of Arabic coffee, a difficult prospect under the best of circumstances, and then: "Turn off the heat, and pay no heed to the rockets. Take the coffee to the narrow corridor and pour it lovingly and with a sure hand into a little white cup: dark colored cups spoil the freedom of coffee . . ."[5]

5.

So what if "nations" are just another way to organize political power which means another way to organize wealth? The "international" must be anyone who moves against this grain, who crosses and recrosses borders, not with allegiance or loyalty to the original idea that physical proximity or natal origin creates intrinsic physical, spiritual or emotional connection that must then be defended with steel or cash, but instead a refutation of that concept and an embrace instead of community through shared values, and an adherence to sustainable and peaceable coexistence with other communities of differing (or similar) values.

I don't think such a place can be seen except through fractured sight, spoken of with a fractured tongue. Because we cannot remove ourselves from our own condition and limitations of awareness, we must live and try to find this place in the actual world. So we are already dependent on the ability of poets to write the future of the society. In her book *In the Heart of the Heart of Another Country*, Etel Adnan writes of Beirut in 1971: "It was a refuge for all sorts of political opponents to the various governments in the region and the matrix for all the tensions that were tearing the world apart . . . In that whirlwind, any living body, human or animal, looked fragile . . ."[6]

You will open me. I am an envelope of flesh. You do not need to open me with bullets or swords anymore. You can open me with invisible rays or by tracking the traces of my physical activity through magnetic wire, cyber-traces. You do not need to graft the technology into me, make me into a cyborg, because I graft myself into the technology. You do not need to make me a machine. I will make the machine me.

The book I use to cross borders, to move from one nation to another, is as good an essay as any about the American experience. On each page of my little passport is a quote relating to the "destiny" of the American project. This "destiny" seems to be endless expansion, expansion without clear purpose. On one page Lyndon Johnson says, "For this is what America is all about. It is the uncrossed desert and the unclimbed ridge. It is the star that is not reached and the harvest sleeping in the unplowed . . . is a new world coming? We welcome it—and we will bend it to the hopes of man."

On another page George Washington suggests, "Let us raise a standard to which the wise and honest can repair." This second quote I cannot see in my own passport because pasted over it is my five-year tourist visa to India.

India, home of my parents and grandparents and my family for at least two hundred years back, has a different idea of "nationality." They began recently issuing status for "Overseas Citizens of India," and the spouses of those same can become "Persons of Indian Origin."

What is the origin of a body of multiplicity, one like mine that was born in England, spent early childhood in India and then was taken to the cold places—first Winnipeg, Manitoba, on the prairies of Canada, then north to Jenpeg, where it snowed in early October and I never saw a deciduous tree. The only Indians I knew were from the Cross Lake Indian Reservation; we bought our fur-lined suede gloves and boots from them. The hydroelectric project my father was working on brought cheap and plentiful power to the city of Winnipeg far to the south, but devastated the local environment. Where are you from, one is often asked. Where indeed? I have no answer

When Etel Adnan returned home to Beirut after seventeen years away she had no way of approaching the task of writing about the return. She instead opted for the form of the short paragraph, borrowed from the book she was reading at the time, *In the Heart of the Heart of the Country* by William Gass. In this book, Gass writes brief entries under various headings including "Place," "Weather," "My House," "A Person," "Wires," "The Church," "Politics," "People" and so on. Sometimes the categories will combine, as in "My House, This Place and Body." In this form of divided intention, Adnan is able to approach— like a Cubist painter, like Gertrude Stein in *Tender Buttons*—the same place, the same people and subjects from a multiplicity of perspectives. Twenty-five years later she rewrites the entire essay three separate times, once about her return to California, once about a time in Libya and the last time, nearly placeless or moving between places.

Adnan, a writer who lives multinationally—in France, Lebanon, California and sometimes in Greece as well—wants to know if the body's experience really *is* tied in any meaningful actualizing way to "locality" (which might or might not mean "nationality?"): "Am I my body and/or my soul, and does an angel define us otherwise? But when I carry pain whenever I'm awake and wherever I go, the question becomes serious. An acute awareness of oneself is not always a blessing." A little earlier she suggests, "the world is somewhere else, in Mexico, in India . . . Why should it always be in a named place? Why should it, altogether, *be*?"[7]

So it may not be somewhere else. It may be within—the experience of the single body inside one's skin. "It's not about history, not about suffering," Adnan insists. "It's not about people, it's about a child gone crazy with power."[8] It is interesting that she positions the idea of "nation" as an infantile one because maybe we could try to develop a model of nationality based on motherhood, a social or political entity whose purpose is nurturing in a certain way the interests and productivity of those people who live within it. Such a nation would have the resources at hand under its own earth available, would belong to the people who live inside it and would have porous borders allowing free traffic between and among other such entities. International popular assemblies might exist to regulate trade and migration between collectives as well as provide education and other human services.

Adnan's folded, refracting and repeating way of exploring the "nation" or "country," is typical of many multinational writers. One cannot choose a single frame or single narrative or single experience. They all happen at once, one after the other, sometimes overlapping, sometimes playing backwards:[9]

> I understand how the muezzin's last call to prayer spreads within the sky and sinks in the direction of the mounting darkness. I'm losing my hold on the sliding day, and sitting on a chair seemingly firm, I feel that I am engulfed by an invisible wave that is carrying me into this geometry we call "the world," and also into something else for which we do not have a name.

In the meantime on the wrong sides of various borders we wait. My sister and her family, having purchased plane tickets, do not receive their visas for travel to India in time for a cousin's wedding. We all theorize it has to do with our father's Pakistani citizenship. He wasn't born there but moved there just before Partition and became a citizen upon the creation of the Pakistani state. When nations—Pakistan, Israel, India—come into existence where there was no nation before, a whole history, a whole nationality, sometimes a whole language, has got to be written, and quickly, to account for it. In groceries stores in the West the large-pearl couscous I learned was a variation on couscous particular to the Palestinians is called "Israeli couscous." Even the marketing of food can be enlisted in the creating of a national consciousness which includes as part of its existence the erasure of the Other.

6.

These nations—most of the new ones of the twentieth and twenty-first century anyhow—received their legitimacy from mandates of European powers. England in particular—and, for an American example, Robert Moses of New York State high-way planning infamy—indulged in the strategy of "partition," brutally effective at separating communities, creating political and social unrest and killing any chance of popular resistance against the mechanism and the machines of empire. In this way "postcolonialism" became a real form of economic colonialism, "post" only the trappings of political empire.

And when the nation is split, people are split from one another and sometimes split inside themselves. Is Adnan's fractured narrative the only solution? In her book *Schizopherene*, Bhanu Kapil explores the connection between migration and schizophrenia. Is a body removed from its nation, its familiar soil, really subject to partition not just of the political sort but inside the brain itself?

The dramatic climax of this poetic dream-essay of a book is the narrative of an incident of domestic violence in the British-Punjabi community. It is between a butcher and his wife and the chorus of neighbors who peek in through the windows of the house (even their criticism of the violence stems from their racism: "*You fucking Pakis, what do you think you're doing? This is England, you bleeding animal*"[10]) are not quite sure they are witnessing a murdering or whether the blood splattered across the dining room table is from the blood-smeared clothes of the family who works at a butcher's shop.

(And me, how am I seen? A "trachea, an alias without sound?"[11] A "signature, bright felon"?)

This confusion of what is seen reflects less on the witnesses and more on the immigrants themselves whose very existence is governed by the inability to perceive or be perceived properly in the new environment. One is reminded of all the Sikh victims of post-9/11 violence, as chronicled and discussed by Jasbir Puar in her book *Terrorist Assemblages*. But one of Puar's main concerns (and we'll return to her in a moment) is to elucidate the ways in which the queer marginalized subject is being un-marginalized, its exclusion from the American polity being undone for the sake of a new support of American economic and political imperial ambitions. Kapil eschews direct political commentary and stays on the level of the social and individual trauma.

In Kapil's case, the trauma is not limited to the subjects of the book but the subject of the "author" herself. Threaded through *Schizophrene* is the story of its writing, or rather the failure of its writing:[12]

> "On the *night* I knew my book *had failed,* I threw it—in the form of a *notebook,* a hand-written final *draft*—into the garden of my *house* in Colorado. Christmas Eve, *2007.* It snowed that *winter* and into the *spring;* before the weather turned truly *warm,* I retrieved my *notes,* and began to write again, from the *fragments, the phrases and lines* still legible on the warped, *decayed* but curiously rigid pages."

It's a good thing Kapil really threw her book into the garden and wasn't just trying to make a further metaphor for the alienation of a subject from perception; I know because on a visit to Naropa University, where Bhanu teaches, she handed me the decayed manuscript itself; I held the book-as-compost object in my hands. She didn't—as she later claims in *Schizophrene*—throw the composted object in the bin when she was finished transcribing what she could from it. Rather she handed it off to Boulder mapmaker and artist Jarvis Fosdick, who created an artist-book/sculpture of the decaying, shredded pages.

Fosdick's object manifests another version of *Schizophrene,* different from the recently published book in standard format. In Fosdick's object, the pages are lashed together in twine and bound between boards covered with text-maps, maps to places that can't be found. The body of the "schizophrenic" is dizzy between localities, unable to place herself. The book *can* be read, but not completely. One must peel away shredded layers to read sentences and phrases written below. In a "Notes" section at the end of the book, Kapil theorizes the benefit of a book in shreds, one she tried to recreate textually:[13]

> From cross-cultural psychiatry, I learned that light touch, regularly and impersonally repeated, in the exchange of devotional objects, was as healing, for non-white subjects (schizophrenics) as anti-psychotic medication. In making a book that barely said anything, I hoped to offer: this quality of touch.

Even this "Acknowledgements and Quick Notes" section becomes a part of the body of the main text. In six short paragraphs, it situates *Schizophrene*, outlines its creation in a learning community of writers and thinkers at Naropa University, describes how its editing process engendered Kapil's next project ("an anti-colonial novel, *Ban*") and a listing of the journals and collaborations (including with Kapil's sister visual artist Rohini Kapil, whose work graces the cover of the book) in which the work previously appeared. These integrative acts seem to serve as the artist/writer's own effort at reversing the damage of mental distress caused by the immigrant condition of migration from familiarity to the new nation, a journey more often than not marked or caused by other stresses—social, political, economic, familial.

The "Quick Notes" section ends with a brief and telling sentence:[14]

> Finally, I would like to extend my gratitude to Olga Visio's *Unseen Mendieta*, a document of Ana Mendieta's *silueta* works that inspired *Schizophrene*, and which I tried to make myself, as close to the border of India and Pakistan as I could get, which was my own mother's garden in Punjab. (73)

So, at last we have a statement of influence, in this case, a statement of absence, the imprint of Mendieta's body, the outline of it, the trace of it. Absence is what makes the condition of a body without nation after all, absence from language, absence from landscape and—no joke!—absence from the food of one's mother and one's mother's people. After all, it is the easiest and the surest sign of the loneliness of the immigrant and that rich smell of curry in the air is the surest sign you have entered an Indian neighborhood or household.

And here also, in the final lines of the book, after the formal "border" of text and "apparatus" has already been crossed, one finds another border, the national border, the one between India and Pakistan. And when Kapil says she made silhouette works in her mother's garden—itself an archetypal place of creation— "as close to the border" as she could get (like my sister and her family, Kapil could not get the stamp of national legitimacy into the book of her passport)—I believe she made them: pressed the skin and flesh of her body into the damp earth.

Body and soil meeting at the close of the book at the "national border" which is a false one—that border in particular, the one that runs through Punjab, the one that separated Amritsar from Lahore, that ripped open the dream of a different nation, Khalistan, one like Palestine which occupied (for the moment) no map—that is the border, soaked with the blood of countless bodies, that could be healed, stitched shut, psychically at least, by the body of the writer-artist, a body-worker herself, pressing herself into the earth.

7.

"It is psychotic to draw a line from one place to another," says Kapil. "It is psychotic to submit to violence in a time of great violence and yet it is psychotic to leave that home or country, the place where you submitted again and again, forever."[15] If the mind itself comes under pressure and duress from the various patterns of forced migrations, what are the coping mechanisms of the immigrant, nearly a monster in the new country, with monstrous customs, deviant sexuality, strange language, strange smells and tastes and clothing.

In the bitter cold of Brampton mid-winter, in the passenger seat of my cousin's car, we watch the old Indian ladies in their saris and parkas and snow-boots striding purposefully from their housing developments to the supermarket. In the fall it is cardigans and sneakers. In the summer it is a light jacket and *chappals*. It is never quite warm enough to wear the sari unaccompanied and, besides, the sari-wearer usually is an older woman, in her fifties or sixties at least, and the skin of her bare stomach and back, revealed by the sari "blouse," really little more than a halter-bra, seems unseemly in the repressed West, just one more reason for her to be seen as monstrous.

Kapil, in this book and in her others, often takes as one of her many departure points the interrogation of the immigrant body as either a monster—an entity unexplainable by and unable to function properly within the social and legal structures of a given society—or a cyborg, a body that, by subvention and subversion, surrenders parts of its own sovereignty to the external processes of the environment around it. In either case it is a body in crisis, one whose very existence and function and processes call into question the efficacy of nationality or nationhood to describe it. In post-9/11 America, the question of the identity or integration of the immigrant's many fractured selves becomes less a question of individual actualization and more a question of actual survival in a social matrix increasingly hostile to the other, in particular the Muslim/Arab other and perhaps ironically and paradoxically the South Asian/Hindu/Sikh other.

In particular, the heteronormative-capitalist practice of control and regulation of queer sexualities extends now to a new "orientalist" framing of the Muslim or Arab body as a "queer" body, a sexually deviant, polygamous, polyamorous, pederastic, pedophiliac body. As Jasbir Puar suggests then, writing about the incidents of pseudo-pornographic photography at Abu Ghraib Prison in Iraq, "not only is the Muslim body constructed as pathologically sexually deviant and as potentially homosexual, and thus read as a particularized object for torture, but the torture itself is constituted on the body as such."[16]

How does a body, a small one, a South Asian queer body, the body of a poet, with a little blue book in his hand cross borders then? Accompanied by verses extolling American expansion, he receives little marks of his legitimacy. A stamp from Uruguay, a stamp from India, and though he doesn't need them, shouldn't need them, stamps from the Canadian government too, and from Spain and France, both countries with open-border agreements with the United States that render visa stamps extraneous. He is annoyed when they stamp—no one else needs this stamp— but grateful for it when he comes home, is separated from his traveling companions, taken to the room in the back, stands there while a stranger runs his hands all over his body. Once he is asked to remove his shirt. Another time he is asked to remove his pants. The weird intersection between sexuality and the apparatus of nationhood and alienation—*his* alienation—is not lost on him. He does flashback, in spite of himself, to the pictures of simulated and actual sexual torture at the prison in Iraq.

I am touching your chest. Your throat. Your stomach. Please unbuckle your pants. Please lower your pants. Please lower the waistband of your underwear. I am touching your groin.

It *does* remind him that here in this place, in every American place, he is less than human. He is reminded that even though he is a citizen, he is—will always *be*—suspect and *a* suspect. And just last week on the news comes information about the CIA's practices of obtaining permission for and carrying out the killing of American-born citizens. So nationality really does only go so far—an adherence and support for a set of political and economic strategies, both formulated and carried out in secret.

And the last page of his passport frightens him. There is a graphic of the earth seen from space—the moon is in the foreground, a satellite floats above—as if to confirm Lyndon Johnson's earlier discourse on America—that its mission is continual expansion, continuing homogenization, that once the Western limit of the continent is reached, the nation will (did) spread out into the Pacific, when once the reaching arms of nationality encircle the planet and meet (they have) they will reach out into space for the star yet unvisited.

Opposite this graphic, in large letters, is the following statement: "This document contains sensitive electronics. For best performance, do not bend, perforate, or expose to extreme temperatures."

Electronics? But where, he wonders, turning the book over in his hands in alarm. True the covers are thick and stiff. *Inside* the covers, he wonders. On the front cover below the "United States of America" there is a small gold square with a circle inside it. Is this chip in the cover underneath that square, he wants to know. And what information is on that chip? About me? Where I have been, which borders I've crossed? Or does it track my movement, track it like the plane on the little screen in front of my seat when I am flying. Now *I* am the one who is being made crazy. As Kapil says, "It is psychotic not to know where you are in a national space."[17]

8.

And anyhow, as a homegrown mama's boy I never had any training for the new role I've been cast in, that of perennial subject. In her examination of the queering of the terrorist subject, Puar goes on to point out that "the fertility of the terrorist (in this case, Muslim men, interpreted through polygamy) and the (homo)sexual perversions of the terrorist, are rendered with extra potency given that the terrorist is also *a priori* constituted as stateless, lacking national legitimization and national boundaries. In the political imagination, the terrorist serves as the monstrous excess of the nation-state."[18] Born monstrous, the suspected terrorist has no national affiliation in the eyes of the first-world powers that he seeks through his extra-state actions to disempower.

And the favorite security questions of the TSA echo back to me at the passport control office of Ben Gurion airport but in my interrogator's broken English: What is you father-name. What is you grandfather-name.

My "father-name" not even real: our family name is Sayeed. Some members of our family spell it "Saeed." We do not agree but only try to approximate by sound. We barely exist at all in English. My father's actual name, Mohammad Asgher Ali Sayeed, wouldn't tell anything about us, migrants for generations—from Egypt to India, from India to Britain, from Britain to Canada. And in the one place of ultimate rootlessness we are the most fixed into otherness. Every male relative of my father's shares the same first name and my father chose to drop the family name. "Kazim" and "Ali" are my two middle names, not my first and my last. So who am I? You can't even begin.

And no one has yet asked me: What is your mother's name.

Maybe it is because the "other," like Athena, is best conceived when sprung full-grown into existence in the shape of the fear one has of it. The other, half-monstrous anyhow, has no mother, is separated from normative practices of sexuality like reproduction, must receive his physical pleasures either through state-sponsored sexual torture or from mystical *houris* in paradise, let alone the vaunted polygamy of Saudi princes or pederasty of Afghan chieftains.

If the science fiction of the '90s explored the ambiguous relationship between human bodies and the technology which was coming to govern their existence—for example *the Matrix* films, the *Terminator* films, etc.—then by 2003's reboot of *Battlestar Galactica*, science fiction was addressing the fear of the queering or non-normalization of the body that attended technology. The essential division between cylon and human is, after all, a trope of queerness: the bodies of the cylons do not participate in the essential heteronormative processes of birth, reproduction, age and death. Immortal, stylish and *brutally* sensual, they are the ultimate Chelsea "clones."

Battlestar Galactica—as the ancient epics like the *Odyssey* and the *Aeneid* were—is a nation-building myth. The twelve human planets have been destroyed by their creations, the cylons, mechanical beings who appear perfectly human in twelve different models and who reproduce by some futuristic process in which the consciousness is downloaded into a new body. Sex, sexuality and parenthood are obsessions that run throughout the series. While the cylons dream of the ability to reproduce biologically (a gift they are willing to sacrifice their ability to transcend death in order to achieve), the humans retreat further and further into a repressive state-controlled sexuality, including banning abortion. The two protagonist characters who are shown to be in same-sex relationships, Felix Gaeta and Gina Inviere, are also both terrorists—Gaeta mounts a mutiny and takes over the ship while Gina detonates a nuclear device aboard the largest civilian vessel in the fleet. The characters' queerness is nearly invisible; it is not revealed in the series proper but in so-called extra features—a series of mini-episodes (Gaeta) that were broadcast on the internet and a stand-alone movie called *Razor* (Gina).

The heart of the series is the construction of new national orders amid the chaos of destruction. The opposite poles of authority—law and justice—are represented by the mother and father figures of Laura Roslin and William. There is a queer perversion of their authority also in the shape of Admiral Helena Cain. She is the ultimate "military man," responsible for civilian massacres, including of her own people, and ultimately ordering the torture-by-rape of Gina, her former lover, now a prisoner.

Of course queer bodies and terrorist bodies, equated in the

narrative, cannot be a part of any "new world order." Having accepted the chore of dying, the cylons do ultimately discover the gift of procreation, though for the human characters too parenthood is similarly vexed. Only one single character has uncomplicated parentage and two living parents. All the other children in the series are depicted as orphans, illegitimate, having single parents, or are in adoptive or otherwise "nontraditional" families. Mother figures (Starbuck, Callie, Athena) and surrogate Mother figures (Laura, Elyosha, Ellen, Caprica Six, Tori) are similarly fraught and normally in crisis. With one single and notable exception they miscarry, fail in their parenting roles, end up mutilated, transformed and/or dead.

Now it makes sense why a little strategically applied slate-blue nail polish couldn't protect me from being profiled as a threat to national order: in creation myths the hyper-sexualized and the effeminate are the most dangerous kind of terrorist—they betray their own kind.

In *Battlestar Galactica,* Ellen, mentioned above, is a complete sexual libertine; she not only enjoys sex, she uses it as well— by literally sleeping with the enemy she is a body that crosses the boundary between the human and cylon enemies again and again, both sexually and physically in her very life and death. Baltar, the other traitor, the one responsible for the original catastrophe, exhibits many outward behaviors traditionally considered feminine or effeminate. In an iconic image from the pilot episode, repeated in the opening credits sequence of every subsequent episode, Baltar manages to escape obliteration via the nuclear blast that levels an entire city of millions of people by— *get this*—crouching in front of his Cylon girlfriend, Caprica Six, his face level with her pelvis, his hands clasping her hips. Later, his treachery finally revealed, bleeding to death, he is saved by Laura Roslin, the ultimate mother figure, when she embraces him tightly, using her very body pressed against his to stanch the flow of blood until help arrives. Baltar, though "straight," sexually effeminate and personally cowardly and craven, is saved over and over throughout the series by strong women exhibiting various mythological aspects of powerful femininity. His final "redemption" in the last episode of the series takes the form of several of the other men in the series grunting humorously in response to his cheekily pointing out the necessary connection between heterosexuality and nation-building.

9.

Technology, whether in service of political empire (the planes flying overheard, bullets that enter the skin) or in service of capital and the relentless and endless consumption that it requires, intervenes in the single unitary body. The Critical Art Ensemble is a group of five media artists who use performance, web installation, scientific experiment and research in order to construct a social and political critique of the role the institutions of science and technology play in our lives. The technology of *vision* in particular, points out the Critical Art Ensemble, has changed not only military reality and capability but has now also infected civilian life:[19]

> Most people have seen the first phases of the civilian cyborg, which is typically an information cyborg. They are usually equipped with laptops and cellular phones. Everywhere they go, their technology goes with them. They are always prepared to work, and even in their leisure hours they can be activated for duty . . . and at the same time can be transformed into electronic consumers whenever necessary.

What place does the individual body or even the individual nation have in a world of constant information-flow? The speed of this information-flow matches the speed of the trading and transference of wealth and resources that is necessary to support the capitalist enterprise. When availability of oil and minerals from the ground diminishes, when the water crisis curtails constant access to freshwater (in so-called first-world countries anyhow; it is already curtailed elsewhere), then the institutions of global economic and political power will move quickly to figure out ways to trademark, restrict access to and capitalize upon even the sun and the wind.

Bhanu presses her body bare into the earth of her mother's garden. As close to the border—the long unmarked border—as she could get. On the other side of India, nearly two hundred Bangladeshi villages surrounded by the Indian border receive no services from either national government. The farmers who live there have no voting rights, no papers with which to travel.

How does a body cross a border? How do borders cross bodies? Meena Alexander writes of returning from a trip to her home and reading a passage from Darwish's *Memory for Forgetfulness*.[20]

> She realizes these words, composed in another place, in
> another language, words written in a time of war translate
> well.
>
> Where she is, migrant memory pitches its tent.
>
> This is her home ground, this borderland of desire and
> meaning making. No elsewhere. (4)

Is that it then? A book as a home, a book to wander with. A book as a passport not the passport as a book. But the book must give us tools then for seeing the individual body against the landscape it inhabits and for seeing the landscape not as political territory, nor for merely its economic possibilities in development but *as a place* itself, with topographical, spiritual and biological values utterly intrinsic and at the same time knitted thoroughly together with the lives and the lifestyles of the biosystem, plant-life, people and animals that inhabit it.

When I was writing *Bright Felon: Autobiography and Cities* I had no intention of writing "poems," or a "book of poems." Perhaps you could say the entire text is a single poem, or reads that way. But I knew in order to write about my life, or more accurately *write my life,* I would have to use not literary form but geographic form, architectural form, specifically in this case, the form of the cities that I had traversed and lived in, even for short periods of time.

Like cities are concatenations of time acting in space (I pointed out once, while giving a walking tour of Walt Whitman's Soho, the buildings that were original to Whitman's time, including the fire-house that was once a bar, a guest-house now a shop and a parking lot once a hospital), my book went sentence by sentence from internal to external, passing through space and time, moving both backward and forward, once discursive, then lyrical, first essayistic then poetic, sometimes all things at once. Someone asked the proper form of it. Part sculpture perhaps, part geometry, part calligraphy because it retains the mark of the writer. Literally on the cover, in the form of orange calligraphy surrounding the subtitle "autobiography and cities." This orange calligraphy is a second secret subtitle, a line of American poetry translated into Urdu and copied there. Usually, even by people who can read Urdu, misread because of the handwriting of the calligrapher, a friend of my sister's who lives in Florida.

Form became critical in the writing of that book because without it—sentences without consequence, one leading into the other, shining into the unexplored and unexamined life: *why had I been silent for so long?*—I would not have been able to manage to speak. The book stutters itself open finally. What begins in clotted and endless sentences opens out into monosyllabics and long vowels. Function follows form sometimes. Someone once said that pentameter is the length of a breath and iambic is the rhythm of pulse. It might be medically true but that is only if you are tuning your fork to two of the many systems in your body, two of the many that exist in the planetary entity, of the many that resound through the cosmos. As Hakim Bey writes of popular music, "the 2/4 and 4/4 beat must be overthrown. We need a new music, totally insane but life-affirming, rhythmically subtle yet powerful . . ."[21]

The map on the cover of *Bright Felon* is by cartographer, artist and DC statehood activist Nikolas Schiller. It is an aerial photo of Lower Manhattan and Brooklyn (the two spindles you see are the Brooklyn Bridge and Manhattan Bridge) refracted and formed into a geometric pattern. It is no mistake it appears as a classical Islamic motif. Some maps are conceptual. In the case of the District of Columbia the question of its political designation is no small thing. A densely populated city, it has a greater population than many Western states that habitually place conservative senators into office. A progressive and politically left community enfranchising these disenfranchised people would swing the entire political balance of the U.S. Senate—and with it national politics—in a new direction.

A map is a dangerous and useless thing, warns Hakim Bey in *Temporary Autonomous Zone*. He says, "The map is a political abstract grid, a gigantic con enforced by the carrot/stick conditioning of the 'Expert' State until for most of us the map *becomes* the territory."[22] But in the actual moment of map-making itself one can find intentions more directly connected to the body—where is the highest point from which to see the terrain around you, where is the closest source of fresh water, where is there shelter from sun or rain. In a world, as Bey points out, in which every square inch of territory, whether land, water or air, on the planet is claimed by some political entity or another, there are critical questions: "How can we separate the concept of *space* from the mechanisms of *control*? The territorial gangsters, the Nation/States, have hogged the entire map. Who can invent for us a cartography of autonomy, who can draw a map that includes our desires?"[23]

10.

In *A Lily Lilies*, poet Josey Foo and choreographer Leah Stein make an effort to map the terrain of the desert landscape of the Navajo Nation. They write that their effort involves "the mapping of spaces through language, of language through movement and of both space and movement through pictures."[24] The book of poems, choreography and photographs presents an interesting new way the abstract of "nation" can be personalized and brought into the individual body.

In the opening poem of the first sequence, "Mound," a woman walks on the earth, sensing it through her feet but always measuring the space around her, the sun "for whom the mound is a texture in the air."[25] She finds the earth she traverses not to be inanimate but the "shape of an ear," in other words, resembling yet another sensing object. She senses the earth beneath her and feels she is received, or sensed back. Stein continues the narrative beneath the poem in her choreographic notes which will run the length of the book *as* subtext and literally *sub*-text: "Words are movement . . . Mappinging—infinite place of discovering . . . The map of the body is infinite."

There is an interactivity between the texts of the poems and the instructions for movement beneath and it is mirrored in the interactions between the bodies of the dancers that is described, as in this note: "She supports him . . . The man and the woman are trees and she is a table, bed and chair."[26] "Their weight is determined by my mind," Foo writes in the poem above. The deeper one travels into the book the more objects lose their boundaries and borders, behave not as nations do but as people do—they pour into one another and sometimes you do not know what you are looking at, textually or actually. One of the traits of the Diné language that Foo plays with is nouns that actualize, become verbs, for example when a lily lilies, or a horse horses.

In one photograph one could be looking at the water, at the sky, at the inside of a mouth—it isn't clear, though you know it is a landscape you are seeing. The parts of the body and the parts of the landscape are not so distinguishable, at least not in the dance. Stein writes, "Contrast between architecture of the body—bones suggesting buildings, kite and ridge—and movement of arms, wrists, elbows, head . . . Arms, wrists, elbows and head seek wilderness."[27] The sensuous forms of the poems in the page imitate biomorphic shapes of eroded tree branches, wind-shaped hills, and the sinuous line of the horizon itself. Dancers become birds, poems become choreography, bodies turn into one another.

This moment—bodies turning into one another—is the moment of "chaos," the moment that precedes most creation myths. It's the moment that Hakim Bey believes needs to be preserved against the interests of "Nation/States," which always require regulation and submission to law in order to increase maximum productivity for the benefit of as few people as possible (in order to maximize the amount of benefit). Bey exhorts, "Don't just survive while waiting for someone's revolution to clear your head . . . act as if you were already free . . . carry your Moorish passport with pride, don't get caught in the crossfire, keep your back covered—but take the risk, dance before you calcify."[28]

146

Words change into themselves, "The sun *shines* but the sun *is* the shine"[29] and dancers change into animals before finally one can be two things at once, "*She is both daughter and river.*"[30] If you can be a citizen of two nations at once—really owe ultimate loyalty to both countries—it could only mean one thing: that war, the most unimaginative and boring methods of resolving conflict, must really be over.

The final sequence of the book, "Imprint," explores the actualization of this contact between physical bodies and the soil of the land, not to possess it nor even necessarily to "learn" from it, but because it *is* and *can be* a productive part of oneself, not as territory to be owned, but as place, nourishment, locality. "I carry a candle to the river/ and acquire my life,"[31] write Foo and Stein, clarified in the volume's final choreographic note, "*Each dancers' movement 'imprints,' becomes part of the other's movement, all movements become one imprint.*"[32]

Perhaps Foo and Stein, who have choreographed site-specific works in train garages, open fields, corner parking lots, vacant city lots, historical sites, gardens and burial grounds, should team up with Bhanu Kapil and create some pieces for all the invisible borders that run under the ground of the American continent, its current political borders so new, so recent not only in the eyes of the Earth but in any conception of human inhabitation here, the borderless borders of the Native communities who predated the establishment of the American political institution.

Bhanu threw her book into the garden to undergo transformative processes, and Foo and Stein talk in their introduction about their book as a "transportable site," hoping it "will travel to very many places."[33] That leaking of the main text in both of these books into what is traditionally thought of as "apparatus"—the index, the notes, the introduction, the biographical data—is exciting because it prefigures an idea about the book as a body, or the book as a nation; a nation could have multiplicity as a founding concept, but such an idea necessarily contravenes the possibility of "empire"—to do away with borders you would have to award ownership of what's in the ground to whoever rightly inhabits that space. Deep in the ground of a book, one thrown into the garden for example, or one constructed in somatic movements in open air for example, one discovers new ways of reading it.

In the "Acknowledgments" section of her own book, Jasbir Puar writes of the death of her younger brother and the beginning of the Iraq War, saying, "It is in between these two scenes of death that this book emanates."[34] She found the two deaths "delicately intertwined," in ways that motivated the thinking and writing of the book. A book—writing—is an *actual* place, resounding with the question of the connection between death and "nation." The body of a nation, after all, is not intrinsic, not permanent; it is, rather, a collective decision to organize politically, with an attendant historiography, cartography and cultural program (arts, literature, performance) to support and legitimize the chosen institution.

So who is the human here then? On the macro-level in a conflict between Nation and individual human body the Nation would always seem to win. Bodies can be pierced, killed, sullied, lied about, suppressed, erased. Nations have a lot of tools, mechanical and otherwise, at their disposal. But I am tempted to say that in a conflict between Nation and individual on a micro-level, the individual always wins. A person is a collection of infinite kindnesses, loves and, indeed, joys. A nation is a fiction, a story everyone has decided to agree is real because it seems either convenient or necessary at the moment.

11.

After all, at the height of the Beirut siege, in fear for their lives, what do Darwish and his comrades do? Listen to the World Cup matches on the radio, obviously. "What is this magical madness that can declare a truce for the sake of an innocent pleasure?" asks Darwish.[35] "What is this madness that can lighten the savagery of war and turn rockets into annoying flies? And what is this madness that suspends fear for an hour and a half, coursing through body and soul more rapturously, even, than poetry, wine, or the first encounter with an unknown woman?"

The "Nation/State" with its machinery of war has an imagination as well, but unlike Darwish, it can imagine only one thing:[36]

The war machine is the apparatus of violence engineered to maintain the social, political and economic relationships that support its continued existence in the world. The war machine consumes the assets of the world in classified rituals of uselessness (for example, missile systems that are designed never to be used, but rather to pull competing systems of violence into high-velocity cycles of war-tech production) and in spectacles of hopeless massacre (such as the Persian Gulf war). The history of the war machine has generally been perceived in the West as history itself . . . Now it has reached an unsurpassable peak—a violence of such intensity that species annihilation is not only possible, but probable. Under these materialized conditions, the human condition becomes one of continuous alarm and preparation for the final moment of collective mortality. (CAE, 54)

If to live, to survive the war machine and its constant demand for more war, more conflict, is to find a nationless place inside, then the idea of a lost homeland, a homeland that doesn't exist on maps but in the imagination, just might be the one that reveals the essential human loneliness and separation from meaningful physical and spiritual experiences that exist in a world governed by greed and motivated by profit.

It is always the human who acts, who transcends the national myth that has been created. Darwish, in his book *Absent Presence,* writes, "Do not look upon yourself in the way they write about you. Do not investigate the Canaanite in you in order to establish that you exist. Rather, seize this reality, this name of yours, and learn how to write your proof. For you are you, not your ghost, the one who was driven away in that night."[37]

The individual must find those zones of liberation "tactile tasty physical space ranging in size from, say, a double bed to a large city," in order to actualize an individual spiritual awakening, one to generosity and kindness, pleasure and the abandonment of "world-hatred and shame," says Bey.[38]

Well it is me, then, with my Moorish passport, refusing to write the laws of the nation on my body but instead to learn through the language of poetry what it really is that binds one human to another in community.

Notes

1. Darwish, *Memory for Forgetfulness,* 6.
2. Darwish, 9.
3. Darwish, 10.
4. Haraway, 133.
5. Darwish, 19.
6. Adnan, xii.
7. Adnan, 42.
8. Adnan, 71.
9. Adnan, 87.
10. Kapil, 49
11. Conoley, 19.
12. Kapil, i.
13. Kapil, 71.
14. Kapil, 73.
15. Kapil, 53
16. Puar, 87.
17. Kapil, 41.
18. Puar, 99.
19. Critical Art Ensemble, 29.
20. Alexander, *Poetics of Dislocation,* 4.
21. Bey, 62.
22. Bey, 101.
23. Bey, 63.
24. Foo and Stein, 1.
25. Foo and Stein, 7.
26. Foo and Stein, 10.
27. Foo and Stein, 24.
28. Bey, 21.
29. Foo and Stein, 3
30. Foo and Stein, 45.
31. Foo and Stein, 50.
32. Foo and Stein, 61.
33. Foo and Stein, 3.
34. Puar, 223.
35. Darwish, 109.
36. Critical Art Ensemble, 54.
37. Darwish, *Absent Presence,* 22.
38. Bey, xi.

Attempted Treasons

Some Notes on Recent Translations

In the note accompanying his recent translations of Hafiz which appeared in a recent issue of *American Poetry Review*, Matthew Rohrer makes the kind of confession that usually makes me immediately suspicious: "I have never read Hafiz in his native language. But the more I read translations, the more I have come to understand that really, honestly, there is no such thing as *the* poem translated from one language to the next. There can't be."[1] For the moment let me set aside my general worry about Hafiz *once again* being translated by a person who by his own admission knows neither the language nor the cultural, religious and linguistic contexts of Hafiz' production, and agree with the general character of Rohrer's statement. Unitalicize his "the," of course, and we would have a disagreement.

Rohrer goes on to quote Matthew Zapruder in saying that despite all the pitfalls and difficulties (and ultimately, that pesky built-in guarantee of failure), a translation can work if it aims to translate the "movement" of energy in the original poem. There is an idea here, probably becoming more popular in contemporary translation, that translation need not worry about the sound or rhythm of the original language, those physical characteristics of language that famously "do not translate," but rather should pay attention to meaning and sense-making mechanisms; in some new translations one sees a greater attention to sentence structure and syntax and grammar of the original language insofar as those things reveal the outline of the mind in motion. Walter Benjamin would be proud: the places the translation fails reveals the actual core essence of the original poem.

"Like a parrot I said/what everyone else said," Rohrer's Hafiz declares, "Roses and weeds/are exactly the same."[2] But for most of us, of course, roses and weeds *aren't* the same and that's the problem, isn't it? If Hafiz is trying to write toward a dissolution of boundaries between an individual and the divine, then Rohrer's translation of the attention to spiritual intent to an attention to more earthy concerns of wine and sexuality may end up bringing that verve of language energy even more clearly to the fore—but such translations undertaken without knowledge of the original language run the risk of missing the mark; of missing a lot of marks. And while it is fine to say then that there should be many translations of a poet, one still must confront the basic fact that the most readily available translations of Hafiz—including these—are all by men who have not read Hafiz in the original.

Roher's translations stemmed from his reading stilted (and to his mind, unpoetic) literal versions made in Iran. He marvels at the physical beauty of the Farsi book he sees the poems in but is "so mad at these terrible English versions of Hafiz." He goes on to claim, "I knew what he was talking about and these poems weren't talking about it. He was talking about getting drunk . . . he was talking about what it feels like to be alive."[3] Once more, let me set aside the quibble that in many Sufi poems of devotion mentions of wine and sex can often be metaphors for ecstatic connection to the divine and not mere "this-world" (to borrow a phrase from Jean Valentine) revelry, and comment instead on the substance of Rohrer's response. He is describing here a moment felt often by readers of translations—including myself—and even poetry in its original language: the moment the reader can see *past* or *through* the limits of language, history and culture to the unbridled and boundless "movements" of human perceptions. If you are reading a poem in an original language (often one you yourself have written) that seems limited in its music or perception, you might well attempt to rewrite it. It seems a natural reaction for a translator to read another's translation and see the places a new translation might illuminate or even return to deep shading.

This is the moment confronted by Christian Wiman in his new translations of Osip Mandelstam, a poet that he—like Rohrer—could not read in the original language. Wiman, however, sought out a native speaker—in this case, Ilya Kaminsky—

and asked him to make transliterations and recordings of the Russian as well as literal trots of several Mandelstam poems that Wiman then set out to recreate in translation. One of Wiman's chief concerns was precisely sound and rhythm and the way the poem moved in its physical shape. He conducted extensive research into Mandelstam's poetics and made many comparative analyses to existing translations.

The poem Wiman calls "To the Translator" is a beautiful example of this attention to sound and rhythm. Where Mandelstam suggests to the translator that eating glass would be equivalent to the chore of trying to translate a foreign language, Wiman writes, "better to bite a light bulb/eat an urn."[4] Wiman stays faithful to the content of the line—as Rohrer says—while trying to ratchet up the sonic qualities to match the Russian. Thus the single line of Richard and Elizabeth McKane, "a strange bird's scream" becomes Wiman's enjambed "sky-wide scream/of a bird we cannot name."[5] Often times, according to Kaminsky in his introduction, the Mandelstam we have come to know *isn't* the actual poet in the original language: another poet has criticized Wiman's extensive alliteration and Kaminsky points out to the friend that Mandelstam's Russian *is* highly alliterative! Wiman is in fact *restoring* those formal properties which had formerly disappeared in translation.

I asked a friend, a poet and translator, about this new Mandelstam. He said something like, "I don't really appreciate these liberal approaches to translation. When I read Mandelstam it's Mandelstam I want to read, not the translator." "But," I said, feeling saucy and perhaps a little irritable, "you *aren't ever* reading Mandelstam. Because Mandelstam wrote in *Russian.*"

Kaminsky, for his part, has been working overtime it seems, to bring the freshness and visceral power of Russian into English. With Jean Valentine he has brought out a book of fragments and poems of Marina Tsvetaeva in which the primary concern is the music and imagery of particular lines and not even the "movement of the mind" through the poem entire. They do not refer to their project as a translation but a "reading" of Tsvetaeva.

Regarding this "reading," W. S. Merwin recalls a moment somewhat like the one Rohrer had with the Hafiz book, after reading Tsvetaeva's poems "a feeling that, vivid and searing though they may have been, she had been in them like a ghost in a cloud, and was gone again."[6] The reader *is* the translator, in cases like these—reaching *through* the words for some sense of meaning or energy.

In one of their excerpts of "Poems for Moscow," Valentine and Kaminsky explore the assonant sounds of the bells: "Seven hills—like seven bells/ seven bells toll in the seven bell towers/ all forty times forty churches, all seven hills/ of bells, every one of them counted, like pillows." Later they describe the "nuns sweeping to mass in the warmth of sleep" and call the riotous citizens of Moscow a "crazy, looting, flagellant mob." The repeating vowels and the liquid sounds of the "L" resonate through the lines to call to mind the ever-present bells. Sound and energy meet here in these powerful sonic shards, carved off the larger poems in Tsvetaeva's work. Not merely the physical shape of the phrases but the energy or movement of the poem entire is compromised in service of the translator's "reading" of the poet in her own language.

Alice Oswald enacts a similar "reading through" in her recent volume *Memorial,* which "translates" *The Iliad* through an accounting, death by death, of the soldiers fallen during the course of the book. This approach to the otherwise-epic gains particular resonance during our current moment of troop withdrawals after a decade-long engagement in the Middle East, during part of which time it was considered unseemly to even list the American dead or show images of their coffins returning. The faceless epic of the war achieves human scale and poignancy when the dead are registered individually, a quality of the conflict that Homer understood full well when he provided biographical details of each soldier killed, including surviving family members and information about his farmlands and estates back in Greece.

Oswald explains her project by saying that it is "a translation of the *Iliad's* atmosphere, not its story."[7] She goes on to talk about its "*enargeia,* which means something like 'bright unbearable reality.' It is the word used when gods come to earth not in disguise but as themselves. This version, trying to retrieve the poem's *enargeia,* takes away its narrative."

She begins her project with the full list of the names of the dead, beginning with Protesilaus, who died leaping from the boats trying to be the first ashore, and ending with Hector, and she finds in each small moment of death the infinity of perception that is the cost of war. And what cost is it to the actual *Iliad* and what Oswald calls her "reckless dismissal of seven-eighths of the poem"?[8]

When it comes to translation—"carrying across" as Odysseus, with Hecabe's complicity, carried the icon of the Palladium across the threshold of the city thus dooming it to fall—Donald Revell finds the practice actually "Edenic."[9] The translator "is a compulsory innocent, incapable of significant harms." After all, Revell opines, "Adam did no harm to the Garden, only to himself." But is that true, after all? If Oswald is heightening our sense of loss and death by removing other parts of the epic and focusing on the individual bodies, does Rohrer's chore of focusing on the wine and wild abandon of Hafiz similarly reveal something missing from the original poem? Or does it conceal? And how do we negotiate the political contexts at work here: Oswald's epic in context of new wars in "Asia Minor," and Rohrer's place in a long lineage of white poets reworking poems of writers from the so-called Middle East according to their own formal and linguistic contexts, a lineage that might also include translators Daniel Ladinsky, Coleman Barks, Edward Fitzgerald and Richard Burton?

Revell says something lovely and fruitful about the mechanics of the translator's task: "Never—call this a caveat—let the issue of mastery of a foreign language discourage or dissuade you from a spell of translation. You and I shall never master English, for heaven's sake, and so what hope have we of mastering a *second* language."[10] It is a fair point; but Wiman, for example, asked Kaminsky's help in sounding out the Russian lines of Mandelstam and engaged in tireless research in order to learn the acoustics of the music he was dealing with as well as historical, literary and cultural contexts. The task of the translator is the task of the poet, true, but it seems the motions of the mind as well as the topography of the words themselves *can* be brought into English.

And as a poet, one hopes, as always, that the bringing of the translated work into English *changes* English, but there is no denying that any translation into Standard English, that global and culturally imperial dialect, has tremendous effect on the original. After all, where *is* Hafiz in the original language, inaccessible even to his own translators?

Redirected from the surrounding events of the *Iliad* in Oswald's *Memorial*, the reader is left solely with death and its aftermath. Of the actual process of translation Oswald says, "I work closely with the Greek, but instead of carrying the words over into English, I see them as openings through which to see what Homer was looking at."[11] This moment of "translation" then incorporates the structure of the poem as a whole as well as its individual lines.

In this sense Oswald's project might be seen more as reinvention, eschewing the general goals of the translator. Oswald, Valentine and Kaminsky, and Rohrer all approach their original source text *as* source text for new creative work, though only Rohrer goes further in his framing of his project *as* translation even while claiming as his very justification the impossibility of the project: "What happens, rather than a translation, is that we get something *like* it, but written by the new person, the translator."

The McKanes' dark Mandelstam warns the translator who seeks to be too faithful to the physical qualities of the original, "In punishment for your arrogance, you incorrigible lover of sounds,/you'll receive the sponge soaked in vinegar for your treacherous lips."[12] But Wiman's Mandelstam knows the truth—like a scheming James Bond villainess who, even while she is threatening Bond with a dire fate, is secretly hoping the suave cad goes ahead with his desperate mission:[13]

So: you, then. Your animal urge. Your primal pride.
To you is given this sponge dipped in vinegar, bitter wad
Of silence: you, who thought love of sound alone could lead to God.

Wiman is as adventurous in his treatment of his source text as Oswald or Rohrer but his intention is to try to move closer to the shape of Mandelstam in the original Russian. Stephanie Sandler, the scholar of Slavic languages who wrote the foreword to Valentine and Kaminsky's Tsvetaeva, said about Wiman's Mandelstam that she could "barely believe that Christian did them without

knowing the Russian and knowing it deeply. And in some po-
ems, the further he goes from the Russian, the closer he comes
to the poem's actual effect."[14]

So how is this different from Rohrer's essaying Hafiz, not
having heard the language? True, Wiman sought intense help
and schooling on the Russian, but his beginning was exactly the
same as Rohrer's: "I 'translated' (I had no resources aside from
other people's translations) a single early eight-line poem to try
to show . . . something I could not find in any existing version."[15]

Rather than the careful and methodical approach of Wiman,
who worked from transliterations and trots by a native speaker
(Kaminsky), nor by Valentine and Kaminsky's approach of col-
laboration, nor Oswald's theorized radical revisioning of the
original, Rohrer worked spontaneously, off the cuff: "I hardly
thought about what I was doing. I wrote out in bald, direct lan-
guage what I thought the poem was about . . . And I kind of liked
this sort of game of wading, late at night, through the writing to
find out what he was really saying. I did ten of them, and then I
went to sleep."[16]

It is possible that their success as poems is precisely due to
Rohrer's state of mind—sleepless, late at night, irritable, alone
with this beautifully illustrated book of "dreadful" poems with
"Faux Victorian verbs ending with–eth"—he leapt forward to
re-write the poems without too much forethought or theorized
intention, done on a lark, in the moment, though informed of
course by Rohrer's own poetic skills and learned attention.

At any rate, it's a risky gambit—one might even say reckless—
but I'm feeling reckless, charmed against my better judgment by
this funny, irreverent, contemporary and American Hafiz.

And as for Rohrer's work as a translator, I'll let his sleep-
deprived god-drunk wonder have the last word:

I have followed him
many times
into the unlikeliest bars

Even hecklers
cannot spoil this fun

Notes

1. Rohrer, *APR*, 25.
2. Rohrer, 24.
3. Rohrer, 25.
4. Mandelstam (Wiman trans.), 39.
5. Mandelstam (McKane and McKane, trans.), 71.
6. Tsvetaeva, 5.
7. Oswald, 1.
8. Oswald, 2.
9. Revell, 61.
10. Revell, 62.
11. Oswald, 2.
12. Mandelstam (McKane and McKane, trans.), 71.
13. Mandelstam (Wiman, trans.), 39.
14. Email to Kazim Ali from Stephanie Sandler.
15. Wiman, in Mandelstam (Wiman, trans.), 73.
16. Rohrer, 25.

Bringing the House Down
Computer Viruses in Anne Carson's Euripides

Anne Carson suggests in her introduction to *Grief Lessons* that tragedy stems from grief and rage, but the real trouble, she seems to point out is that you *can't* have a "grief lesson." The pun meant to perhaps reassure, doesn't because *does* grief lessen? Unlikely.

And after all, what is it you can ever learn about the body? Inside it you think you will never die. That's the real tragedy: that a couple thousand years after these plays what galls is not that the joke's on *you* but that the joke's *on* you. That's the reason Herakles brings the house down *every time*, while you, the audience member, who has seen the play a hundred times, keep rooting around for the dramatic tool which might prevent him from the act. As if you could call out into the empty space that separates you (as a single member of the "audience." Singular of "audience" being "audient." Suddenly no longer a passive receptacle of an entertainment but something graver) from all the action in the universe.

Which, in the Greek, classically, of course is barely action at all.

Anne Carson stages her drama as if it were a selection of four plays, a four-act tragedy. And, as with the best of Euripides, the real action happens in the spaces between what the audience sees on stage; in this instance, in the brief essays between, Carson pretends to write an explanation but instead creates an extension of the tragedy.

But I question her—what? Not motive—her melancholy.

Because while she presents first what she purports are the roots of tragedy—first rage, then grief—what she uncovers through the course of the four plays is the odd in the epic, that creepy fact of the funny amid the horror, that "trembling of laughter, terrible if it broke out."[1]

Information is power: we know that in our digital age. It perhaps explains our continuing interest in Euripides. His plots revolve around information: who has it and what they do with it—especially that their use of misinformation can ruin a marriage, cause a miscarriage or even start a war. Stratified by class, only characters who can manipulate information properly can manage to transcend their social situations.

In Theseus' case, in *Hippolytos*, it costs him his son. In Admetos' case in *Alkestis* it may or may not have brought his wife back to him from the land of the dead. Euripides himself is cagey about it (the resurrected woman does not speak) and Carson chooses to highlight that lack of clarity in both her introduction and in the translation itself.

What people do and don't know about the lives of their companions and how they communicate or miscommunicate that information is one of the primary plots of Carson's Euripides. Like its contemporary counterpart *Downtown Abbey,* Carson's *Grief Lessons* haunts the house with the aftermath of messages gone astray, friends unfriended and lurkers catfishing, not solely to land a mate (who *is* that woman at the end of Alkestis?), but, in Hekabe's case, for more brutal revenge.

"To live past your myth is a perilous thing," runs the tag line of Carson's newest book *Red Doc>* which revisits her star-crossed couple Geryon and Herakles from *The Autobiography of Red.* The sunny and beautiful Herakles has become a sad, PTSD-afflicted shell of himself. But in *Grief Lessons* he is a "cliché," having just arrived back from the land of the dead, he is unbeatable, "perfect."[2] Not for long. Carson highlights in her essay the dividing moment in the middle of the play. She even suggests that once it happens, "You may think it's over and head for the door."[3] Then all hell breaks loose.

Carson calls more attention to the moment of division when she talks about Admetus' partitioning of his house in order to accommodate Herakles' carousing during the funeral of his wife in the final play of the book, *Alkestis.* But now we are looking into the future, which is a tricky thing and it is always good to remember that vague knowledge, in Carson's universe as well as in Euripides', is generally ill-advised.

Carson takes care to describe the physical shape of the stage and where the players are. Her idea is that the Greek plays are a form of moving sculptures, a set of tableaux, that the main characters are going through *motions* of a tragedy everyone watching *already* knows is coming. What's interesting then, to the audience, is how the chorus *processes information.*

Caught between the divine gods who make his fate and the chorus who *make it real* by uttering it—if it's not on the internet it didn't happen, goes the contemporary media creed—Herakles, in what Carson identifies as a postmodern move, turns his back on both. "Bold move," she concedes admiringly, "Perhaps he is a tragic hero after all."[4]

Carson strips the dialogue of characters down to information. Poetry she leaves to the chorus. There is something musical and terrible, of course, in the plain way her characters utter pithy lines at each other.

Herakles has nothing else to live for at the end of the play, having killed his entire family in bloodlust. But he no longer believes the gods drove him to tragedy: "I don't believe gods commit adultery. I don't believe gods throw gods in chains. Never did believe it, never shall."[5] He decides to go on with his life.

"We go in pity, we go in tears," moans the chorus at the close of the play.[6] What they've lost is not their friend, but their idea of the hero, blessed or even cursed by gods.

Echoing that closing phrase, Beckett's Vladimir asks, "Shall we go?" in the epigraph to Carson's preface to the next play, *Hekabe.* Beckett guides not only her structuring of the dialogue but also her perception of the bleakness of Euripides—"Why is Euripides so unpleasant?" she asks. "Certainly I am not the only person who thinks so."[7]

She goes on to quote Beckett on the question of tragedy: "Tragedy is not concerned with human justice. Tragedy is a statement of an expiation." Hekabe, like Herakles, breaks down during the course of the play that bears her name. Unlike Herakles, she does not act in the madness of chaos but with cold-blooded premeditation.

No coy dropping of soap in a slippery high-traffic spot so the mistress of the house slips, as in a crucial *Downton Abbey* plot twist—rather, Hekabe goes straight for the kill. In contrast to the Greek masculine ideal of Herakles, who ends the play as a huddled mass, this Trojan woman begins the play broken and powerless but, as Carson says, soon "rises up, assembles herself one last time to action." In response to her prophesied punishment—the aforementioned transformation into a dog—she seems unconcerned. Carson explains, "Her suffering for the original sin of having been born is already off the human scale. Really there is nowhere for her to go but out of the species."[8]

Still, it is not only Hekabe's lack of traditionally "heroic" qualities nor the weird structure of Euripides' plays that disturbs Carson, rather it is her Beckettian embrace of the fact that these plays, unlike the bulk of the Greek corpus, lack a "clear moral issue." Unlike Iphigeneia in Aeschylus or Antigone in Sophokles, whose deaths "change the stories in which they are set," the deaths in Euripides, to Carson, feel "muffled," or even to have "irrelevance" to the story at large.[9]

It's quite a claim, considering many of Euripides' women—Hekabe here, but in other plays Hermione, Medea, Agave and so on—are murderous if not actual murderers. She attributes this quality to the period of endless wars Euripides was writing in, the collapse of the empire of Athens, "not to say the cultural moment we call 'classical Greece.'"[10]

If anything Hekabe seems neither to act based on the immediate revelation of Polyxena's death, nor that of Polydorus. Earlier in the play when Polyxena bids farewell in absentia to her brother Polydorus, Hekabe remarks "If he lives. I am doubtful. My luck nowadays is not good."[11]

Also unlike immortal Herakles, Hekabe is eager for death and enraged when she is denied it. When she is brought the corpse of her son, betrayed by an ally, she does go through the motions of grief, but finally admits, "I was not wrong."[12]

The dog-woman loses her argument with Menelaus in a similar trial-like debate over Helen's fate in Euripides' equally distressing *Trojan Women,* but in this play bearing her name she is able to use her crafty tongue to sway Agamemnon into, at very least, looking the other way while she plans her revenge. "Shit. No mortal exists who is free," she very reasonably points out to him. "Slaves to money or fortune or the city mob or the written laws—none use their own mind!"[13]

Regardless, there's no victory for Hekabe. She prevails in the trial at the play's conclusion but cares not, and nor, in this case, does the chorus. Rather than deliver a final summation and coda to the play's lesson, they just slouch off stage muttering, "Now we taste the work of slaves. Hard is necessity."[14]

Neither Hekabe, Agamemnon, nor the chorus remark on the truly important event at the close of *Hekabe*—after Polymestor is denied justice for his children's murders and his blinding, he begins to shout all he knows of the futures of the defendant and the judge, information revealed to him by others. He speaks of Hekabe's canine transformation, the betrayal and murder of Agamemnon, the killing of Kassandra—he spills it all out onto deaf ears while being dragged off stage by the Greek prison guards as Agamemnon shouts him down and Hekabe waves a dismissive hand, completely unconcerned with the future now that her revenge has been served. As Carson tartly summarizes, "With her new shopping cart Hekabe, Queen of Troy, will be prowling the aisles for dog biscuits."[15]

Of course ignoring crucial information or misusing it is what Euripidian characters excel at, so it is no surprise when Theseus so badly misconstrues what is happening in his own house in the third play Carson translates, *Hippolytos*. In the introductory essay she explores the connection between sexuality and shame and the way that plays out for Theseus, his wife, Phaidra, and her stepson Hippolytos. In this case the mere perception (Phaidra's, Theseus') drives events more directly and powerfully than anything that actually happens.

After all, if it's on the internet it must be true.

What complicates matters here are three things: first, Hippolytos' own inability to reconcile a healthy spectrum of sexual expressions; secondly, the untranslatability of the Greek work "polle," which Carson tries to explain as "muchness"—a quality of "access that cuts across certain lines of morality or moral sentiment we might prefer the gods to respect"; and finally the fact that Phaidra herself is "a tricky soul to capture, apparently" in that Euripides wrote two plays about her, the first no longer extant. Of it Carson says only nineteen short fragments and guesses that the first play "may have depicted an aggressive and lascivious Phaidra."[16]

Phaidra holds in between the two plays both sides of the sexuality that Hippolytos cannot grasp in either case. His inability to process this information renders him relevant not as a human body but as a mere bit of programming—a concept. Aphrodite sets in motion the program to delete the body while Artemis programs the concept into the wedding rituals.

And for her part, Phaidra, like most of the corpses that litter Euripidean stages, is just a bit of pretty scenery.

But that is only part of what is interesting here. The other part is that all of this is happening in the house of Theseus, the man who appeared to offer Herakles safe harbor after that hero killed all of his own family in his god-driven madness in the first play of Carson's book. He, like Herakles, at a critical moment refuses divinity. "Without any test of oath or pledge or oracle, without trial, you'll cast me out?" cries Hippolytos upon being accused of violating Phaidra. "No need for divination!" replies Theseus. "Let the birds of omen fly over my head—be gone!"[17]

And then Hippolytos appeals to someone better than the gods: "O house! If only you could speak for me, bear witness!"[18] In the age of pure information, we want more than anything to *be* somewhere, to belong to a place and for that place to be *real*. It may be why it is so interesting for people to use their electronic devices to "check in" and post "status updates," to mark the times and places of their lives.

The setting itself becomes an organizing principle by which the hapless characters therein can moor themselves to something real. In the end it is not the king but a slave who is able to see truth for truth and proclaim belief in Hippolytos' innocence even in the face of mounting circumstantial evidence. He is not heeded. It's Euripides' cruel quirk that even after proof of their uselessness in affecting human affairs he still brings gods in at the end to tidy up the dramatic mess. Theseus is finally set aright by the sudden appearance of Artemis, who explains everything.

In the end, it is the gods who become irrelevant. First Hippolytos as a ghost gives his father an out to weasel out of guilt—"Yes I was deluded by gods," Theseus agrees in response to his son's opening gesture—and then he directly absolves him: "I free you from this murder."[19]

It's this kind of train wreck of the ideals of "justice" and "order" that were such foundational aspects in the earlier plays of Aeschylus and Sophokles that makes Euripides so "unpleasant" (in Carson's words) and she seems committed to exposing and highlighting that side of him.

The final play included here, *Alkestis,* was originally performed in place of a satyr play and it fulfills the same role in Carson's collection. Definitions "blur" and the main plot details seem to fluctuate. Admetos has made some kind of deal with Death to have his wife die in his place. No one is clear on the terms of the deal and when it happens Admetos seems blindsided by his grief, though Carson is quick to point out that he is making "free use of clichés of lament." As if the situation itself isn't bizarre enough on its own, enter Herakles.[20]

He brings with him the second reason to mistrust Anne Carson, whose craft and craftiness both mark these translations. Is one to understand this jocular, hard-partying Herakles as existing chronologically before the slaughter of his family in the opening play? Or has his madness utterly disappeared? It matters because, while Carson has opened her collection with the dissolution of Herakles, continued it with the crumbling of his guardian Theseus, and closed it with this completely surreal picture of the put-together and capable hero back in prime form (translating death into life is not for the weak of will), the plays were actually written and performed in antiquity in *reverse order.*

Dating Euripides is a tricky business, my colleague Kirk Ormand warns me, but it's generally accepted that *Alkestis* was performed in 438 BCE followed by *Hippolytos* in 428 BCE and *Hekabe* just a few years later, around 425–424 BCE. *Herakles* is harder to date, Ormand says, but it seems likely the play was written and performed much later, as early as 424 or, more likely, as late as 416 BCE. Ormand says, "the later dates are based on a stylistic analysis of meter, and a tendency of Euripides to use certain metrical patterns with increasing frequency in later plays."[21]

Of course, by now Carson's audience, unlike Hippolytos, has learned how to read nonlinearly and understand all conditions—including the tragic and the comic—to exist nearly at once. Though the house itself is partitioned physically here, partitions in general—including that between Herakles' madness and sanity—are made, by Carson's placement of the plays, to seem completely arbitrary in the end. This effect of "jarring comic and tragic effects against one another" is a key Carson strategy in the translation of Euripides.[22]

As mentioned before, the conclusion of this play—like Euripides' anti-dramatic conclusions to his plays *Medea, Helen* and *The Trojan Women*—seems to work against conventional structure: the rescued woman returned from the dead remains anonymous, does not speak. Admetos begs Herakles, heroic normalizer, to stay on as a guest. Perhaps he is hoping that Herakles' presence will undo some of the weirdness surrounding the ambiguous transcendence of death?

It doesn't matter; Herakles begs off in the most dismissive way—"Another time. I have obligations."—and splits.[23]

In the end, it seems that Carson always wanted to write against expectation: to find the dry horror in the everyday, the nearly funny in the dreadful. The key aspect of a tragedy for ancient audiences was always a rehearsal of an inevitable chain of events coming to pass, but in these plays by Euripides, the gods are tools, dumb as rocks, and it's really the wily who know how to navigate the chaotic overflow of information and sensation that is the human condition. Herakles seems completely casual in *Alkestis* about transcending death, as equally blasé as Hekabe is about her impending canine transformation.

After all, information *isn't* always power. Ask Polydoros. It is chilling indeed—"unpleasant" as Carson says—that the university may grind on by purely mortal will, headless and heartless.

As the chorus mumbles at the close of *Alkestis*, "What we imagined did not come to pass—God found a way to be surprising."

Notes

1. Carson, 249.
2. Carson, 13.
3. Carson, 14.

166

4. Carson, 17.
5. Carson, 79.
6. Carson, 84.
7. Carson, 89.
8. Carson, 90.
9. Carson, 92.
10. Carson, 93.
11. Carson, 119.
12. Carson, 130.
13. Carson, 138.
14. Carson, 159.
15. Carson, 97.
16. Carson, 167.
17. Carson, 223.
18. Carson, 224.
19. Carson 239–241.
20. Carson 247–248.
21. Email to Kazim Ali from Kirk Ormand.
22. Carson, 247.
23. Carson, 306.

Old School

Lalla, or Lal Ded, was a Kashmiri mystic who lived in the fourteenth century at the height of Kashmiri Shaivism. Though she was a Hindu and a yogi, even Shah Hamdan, the great Sufi teacher who was her contemporary, recognized her as a saint. The best translations are those of Indian poet Ranjit Hoskoté, who worked directly from the old Kashmiri, and who incorporates into his translations the inconsistencies of style and diction and textual variations that stem from the nature of these ecstatic utterances passed down by word of mouth over the course of centuries before being assembled into a written canon.

Here's a short verse:[1]

I'm towing my boat across the ocean with a thread.
Will He hear me and help me across?
Or am I seeping away like water from a half baked cup?
Wander, my poor soul, you're not going home anytime soon.

Here Lalla is either pulling her vessel (her body?—but if the vessel is her body then who is doing the pulling?) *through* the water or she herself is the water? At any rate, it seems not to matter, either to the nameless He (one presumes it is God) because she enjoins her soul (not her body, her *soul*) to continue to wander. It's a lot of thinking packed into four short lines, far indeed from the palliative and pithy epigrams one has become used to in spiritual literature.

Indeed, Lalla explores a fragmentation of the self that feels typical in contemporary discourse, but at the time the great philosophers of yoga were only beginning to wonder what the nature of the individual human self was. In Lalla's poetry the question was never simple and never resolved:[2]

He who strikes the Unstruck Sound
calls space his body and emptiness his home,
who has neither name nor color nor family nor form,
who, meditating on Himself, is both Source and Sound
is the god who shall mount and ride this horse.

Gods and humans seem equally confused, equally desirous of
knowing their own natures. In another short verse Lalla skewers
secular life as well as the yogis and Muslims who practiced their
own kinds of asceticism[3]:

Gluttony gets you the best table in the town of Nowhere,
fasting gives your ego a boost.
Slaves of extremes, learn the art of balance
and all the closed doors will open at your touch.

What Lalla called for, in her poetry, was a turning away from re-
ceived knowledge and the institutions of religious thought and
an embracing of an experiential learning based on the sensory
knowledge of the body in its many and varied physical forms.

Most importantly, Lalla deviated from the prevailing Vedanta
philosophy at the time which held that *Brahman*, the creative
energy of the universe, was inactive and that the entire uni-
verse was *maya* or illusion. Lalla instead subscribed to Kashmiri
Shaivism, which held that the entire existing universe of matter
and energy (*Shakti*) was a manifestation of universal conscious-
ness (*Shiva*), real and eternal.

But is it still interesting to try to think about the relationship
between "matter" and "spirit?" Which could mean "Shakti" and
"Shiva" or "earth" and "heaven," as you like? The humor and
whimsy of the spiritual poetry makes sure the work is always on
the reader, always on the practitioner to continue to think and
search, not in an abstract way but in the actual physical world.
Because if it isn't just illusion, or a temporary world waiting to
be dissolved in favor of a promised "afterlife" or vision of Bibli-
cal "heaven," then what's in the world, its blessings and failures,
actually *matter*. A spiritual practice of yoga is not separate but is
the same as a life lived in solely material terms.

Here is a verse that deals with this issue and also demonstrates some of the exciting shifts in diction that would not look out of place in a journal of contemporary poetry[4]:

> Now sir, make sure you've corralled your ass.
> Or he'll champ his way
> through your neighbors' saffron gardens.
> No one's going to stand proxy
> when it's your neck on the block.

Lalla's poetry puts me in mind of the childhood game of Hide-and-Seek, because when you are selected as unique—the only one in the universe—you are alone, abandoned by all the other players. You hope to touch them while they evade you and head back to God. You are alone with God in only one case: before you start your endless search. There you are, crouched down, completely ignorant of the wide world around you because your hands are over your eyes.

But in just a moment you will be allowed to Seek.

Count to ten. Ready or not. Here you come.

Notes

1. Hoskoté, 6.
2. Hoskoté, 81.
3. Hoskoté, 84.
4. Hoskoté, 85.

Translation Is a Trick

The kind you turn. Your turn it because you want to make love to a stranger but you still want to get paid, either in money or jewels or another poem in your pocket you can run away with.

I translated Ananda Devi because I wanted to *write* those poems. So sometimes it is a jealous trick. I chose her book *quand la nuit consent à me parler* because it was small and its cover was hot pink with yellow lettering. But as I read the poems I knew I couldn't ever have written poems so raw, so honest, so *angry*.

But I couldn't translate them in Paris where I found the book. It took my arrival in Pondicherry in francophone India to start to see the poems as mine. And it took three more weeks and my arrival in Varkala, on the shore of the Arabian Sea, to feel the rhythm of Devi's ocean-borne Mauritienne poetics.

Poetry finds a place in the poem. Donald Revell argues that you can't find poetry in poems; it's likely true, but you *can* find poetry in translations, more than in writing poetry because in the translation you, the poet, are watching it happen.

Here is one line of Cristina Peri Rossi's book-length poem of fragments and scraps, called *EVOHE*:

Una mujer por poesia poseida

A woman by poetry possessed? As if. Here is the famously "untranslatable," not just because there is no way to fake the slip of the tongue—and it *is* in the context of this poem a cunnilingual erotic slip of the tongue as well as a very cunning lingual one— but the character of the Spanish labial consonant "p" isn't sexy in English but crude.

Anyhow, I had enough lost opportunities in other places in Peri Rossi's book to get at her sauciness and her combining of

171

biblical and pornographic dictions—so I made a quick switch out here and solved my problem:

A woman by poesy possessed.

It's a cheap shot, to be sure, but it works. Taking the "t" out of "poetry" really smooths the line down to sexy. Poesy may be old fashioned but in context it's a little dirty. No one said solving translation problems always had to be hard. Sometimes you just have to be a little brazen.

It brings me to my most recent translation project, Sohrab Sepehri, an Iranian poet who wrote in Farsi, a language I neither speak nor read. When my father went to Iran for work I asked him to bring back to me volumes of contemporary Iranian poetry. I had grown up listening to the Arabic recitations of scripture and the Urdu poetry and mourning songs commonly recited during the month of Moharram, but though one of my grandmothers was Iranian I was unfamiliar with the contemporary poetry of that place.

Among the books my father brought back were volumes by Sohrab Sepehri. They had been translated but the poetry of the lines felt stilted, formal, prosaic. I was taken with one line though: "I am a Muslim! The rose is my *qibla!*" The *qibla* is the direction of worship toward Mecca. Observant Muslims will turn in this direction wherever they are in the world. In hotels across the Muslim world and in South Asia this direction is marked by a large arrow painted on the ceiling. The fact that Sepehri was declaring not Mecca but a simple rose to be his *qibla* struck me to the core.

Since I could not read the Farsi myself, I worked with Mohammad Jafar Mahallati, my colleague at Oberlin. He would read the lines and then translate them on the spot for me. I would take notes on the earlier translation, then use his comments and clarifications to assemble the poem, make notes, and read my rendition back to him. He would stop me, elaborate, we would discuss, debate, argue. Eventually we would have a poem.

Sepehri in Persian is two things at once: very plainspoken, *prosaic* even, and then incredibly deeply philosophical and abstract. A poem about shopping for pomegranates turns into a poem about the impossibility of knowing the physical world at all. A poem about fish in a pond turns into a reflection on the element of water and then on the tragedy of the separation of human from the divine. No one thing is another in Sepehri's world, yet these observations are tossed off in the most casual language. It *is* hard in English to keep up.

As we worked on "Water's Footfall," the poem from which the above line came, and then on other Sepehri poems, we found ways to render the language in a lyrical and musical way that matched the stark plainness of the original language. But I never could improve upon the bare declaration "The rose is my *qibla*" and so kept that phrasing in our rendition. How could we have translated that word "*qibla*" without diminishing its power in the explanation? We bet on the fact that with increased relationships between cultures eventually the word would find its way into English and in future editions it may not even require italics. And anyhow, it's not a precise translation of the original Farsi line which reads "*Man musulman. Qiblam ek ghul sourgh*" or "I am a Muslim. My *qibla*, one single red rose." We both found our sparer line closer in spirit to the bare daring of Sepehri's sentiment than the closer translation, which seemed somehow too lush, too personal. Also, in English syntax the line would require that comma (or a colon) which graphically interrupts the declaration.

There is a space between humans and god, after all, which does not translate across languages. What could Sepehri have meant? Translating means to carry words not just across languages and cultures, but often through time itself.

The *Iliad* as translated by Stanley Lombardo, for example, is brutally contemporary. I say brutal because we know well what it is like to live through ten years of what seems to be endless war. But the war is long in coming in the epic. It opens with the disagreement in the Greek camp, continues with the litany of the ships and then strangely, fabulously, the scene switches to Troy. Helen joins the elders on the walls and points out the various characters among the Greeks. But below them on the field, the men have had it with fighting. They come up with a sensible plan to pack it all in and send everyone home. (It took them ten years to figure this out? Of course it did.)

But history is not to be foiled. While the men agree their war is to be settled on a single combat, Aphrodite spirits Paris away at his moment of defeat. Aphrodite approaches Helen and demands she comfort Paris, safely ensconced in the royal bedroom. Helen refuses.

Aphrodite, of course, is a goddess not to be trifled with nor questioned. "Wretched girl," warns Lattimore's goddess, "do not tease me lest in anger I forsake you." But Lombardo's Aphrodite is a little stronger, a little more in control of her situation. "Don't vex me, bitch," she snaps menacingly, "or I may let go of you."

Small wonder Helen complies.

The trick of translation is that the act of it transforms everyone: the original text, the new language, the author and the translator all. Working on Devi and Peri Rossi's very different engagements with the body changed my own poetics. Sepehri and Marguerite Duras, whom I have also translated, affected my rhythm and diction in English.

I asked Stanley Lombardo once how he came up with such a beautiful and radical departure to have Aphrodite so freshly menace Helen. He laughed. "It's not a departure," he said. "It's exactly what it says in Greek!"

When I completed the Sepehri translation I sent it to my friend Navid and his father both of whom had read Sepehri in Farsi and loved him. Navid wrote back that both he and his father loved the translation but they worried about one single line, the poem's most famous line, which is (of course) "*qiblam ek ghul sourgh.*" They felt that the line was meant by Sepehri as very tongue-in-cheek, a little sarcastic almost, that he was being ironic when he said "I am Muslim," that it was not an earnest declaration as I had read it.

But there was something so true in me when I thought of him saying in full earnestness, "The rose is my *qibla*," claiming that part of the natural world as a true direction of worship. He goes on in that same part of the poem to say the stream is his prayer rug, that his mosque is a meadow, that his Ka'aba (the great black cubical mosque in Mecca) is the wind in the trees.

In the end I took a chance.

Pythagorean Poetics

Poetic language to me *means* to become strange and veer from normative use. As in prayer speaking in tongues because G-d is both unspelled and unseen. Would be unseemly to actually speak Hir name. In Islamic tradition, of course, G-d hath no name: 99 of them OK but really the "hundredth" name—a metaphor not a name—is unspeakable, unknowable. "Allah" is not a word but a contraction: of "Al-ilah," "ilah" meaning only "god" (lowercase), or, pedantically, "something one worships." Usually when I type "worship" out of habit my fingers type instead "workshop." In both a session of "worship" and a session in the "workshop" a thing gets *made*, not revealed but made.

So to the spasmed light-licked fractured sentences or phrases that would make a poetic line: collection of lines with musical or ideational intent means a "poem," a text or textile—the way threads woven give you something to wear or cover yourselves with. But the poem as a text to me is intentional or not, as opposed to prose, which requires intention and even if the author does not intend, such intention will itself reveal.

American language has suffered the same way the American body has—by our compulsion toward empire, co-opting and colonizing and suppressing and murdering on a grand and global scale. We can hardly say anything or move anymore without cutting ourselves to the bone. We move toward strangeness and wildness in our expression not so much as a political gesture (for most) but as a way of finding a zone free of commercialism and untainted by political and military institutions. But sometimes it seems that all we have is *information*. As Kenneth Goldsmith writes of the new trend and tendency toward repurposing language, "Far from this 'uncreative literature' being a nihilistic, begrudging acceptance—or even an outright rejection—of a presumed 'technological enslavement,' it is a writing imbued with celebration, its eye ablaze with enthusiasm for the future . . ."[1] Is that really the case? A future obsessed with mere rehashing and quoting and putting work in new context? Goldsmith points out that this is how literature has always built itself—by ransacking its own historical archives. He may be correct, but it feels like a conservative point of view to me in light of the knowledge that still lies unearthed in the body's stores.

And I'm not sure I want his "spectacle of the mundane," anyhow. Though as he points out, this writing is *not* without "emotion": "far from being coercive or persuasive, this writing delivers emotion obliquely and unpredictably, with sentiments expressed as a result of the writing process rather than by authorial intention." Maybe I could buy that.

At any rate, I have a hard time reconciling any "idea" about writing with what and how I write because the task itself is a dreadful one. I sit in the wind or stunned somehow in the afternoon and write some sentences on a piece of paper, which more often than not I will lose. Is writing loss? If there is no word for G-d, there's no word for anything I am sometimes afraid.

No one hears in the dark, no audience. No wish for wonder, no god to answer your prayer, your pot breaks itself under hands on the wheel. But the "lyric" mode for me is the snake that sings through me, from whom I will accept any apple. Because it depends on strings. Music and sound vibrations are the foundational essence of the extant universe—it might be an aesthetic point of view but it also happens to be a statement about the physical makeup of the universe as we now understand it.

So rather than either the concept or "revelation"—some angel who whispers in your ear, Mister William Blank—or finding and manipulating data as Goldsmith or Abramson or others do—maybe you just have to *listen hard*. The first thing you ought to hear is what's closest: heartbeat and breath. In discussing the way blind people listen, Stephen Kuusisto uses the term "creative listening." He explains that "Blind people are not casual eavesdroppers. We have method. As things happen around us we reinvent what we hear like courtroom artists who sketch as fast as they can." He refers to his perceptions as both "clear and improbable": "Even when I listen to Manhattan traffic I'm drawing my own pictures of New York—the streets are crowded with Russian ghosts and wheels that have broken loose from their carriages."[2]

Pythagoras knew it all along, knew that one must tune oneself to external resonances, that there existed mathematical equations that could map the mysterious dimensions of creation. For him distances between distant planetary bodies in the sky were related to the tones in between notes on a musical scale. Such weaving together of matter in the physical universe is the province of poetry. Imagine Jorie Graham in her poem "Steering Wheel," her hands on the steering wheel, looking in the rearview mirror in order to back out of the driveway. Leaves rise up in a swirl of wind, a hat blows down the street. A quote on Oppen springs to mind. It all comes together or does it really in "the part of the law which is the world's waiting/and the part of the law which is my waiting,/and then the part which is my impatience—now; *now?*"[3]

In her early book *The End of Beauty*, Graham is skeptical of our ability to live without "being seen" by the outside. She wonders of Adam and Eve, after being abandoned, "who will they be, dear god, and what?"[4] Yet in her later book *Swarm* she comes to know of God, "In His dance the people do not move."[5] We become fixed in place, undeveloping, when we rely too much either on our history or our preconception. *Swarm* is full, rather, of imperatives and open-ended imperatives at that: "Explain asks to be followed/Explain   remains to be seen."[6]

And so, like Pythagoras with his math and music (and perhaps not coincidentally the vow of veganism that all members of his learning community had to make), we fall back on careful observation not just of our own bodies but their relationships to all other bodies and functions in the universe—those very close (the food we put in our bodies) and very far away (galaxies and cosmic phenomena). As Goldsmith points out, "The secret: the suppression of self-expression is impossible . . . the act of choosing and reframing tells us as much about ourselves as our story of our mother's cancer operation."[7]

Interesting or ironic or both that Goldsmith's metaphor for the most revealing of personal subjects for poetry is the illness of one's mother. I'll refrain from too facile a discussion of either eco-disaster or existential angst at alienation from the abandoning God. Instead let me choose the third prong—our organic bodies, weak and mortal (how dare they die?), now in the very process of being subsumed and trumped by technological machinery that can "live," they are so much more capable than we are in their sensory perceptions and their ability to intake, process, manage and distribute information.

We do one thing only that machines don't: breathe. In that experience (and its metaphorical extensions) we *actually* physically interface with the matter of the universe. Maybe it is true that no god exists in the dark, that there is no audience for prayer. But another human could suffice, and not through a machine but a voice in strings into an ear a box. A body is an *instrument* and it has registers yet untested.

"You are inside me," says Graham, "as history./We exist."[8]
Meet me.

Notes

1. Goldsmith, 5.
2. Kuusisto, ix.
3. Graham, *Dream of the Unified Field*, 161.
4. Graham, *End of Beauty*, 3.
5. Graham, *Swarm*, 12.
6. Graham, 5.
7. Goldsmith, 9.
8. Graham, 105.

Ode to Silence

Lecture Notes

Kinds of silence in poetry:

- –pauses in a line, silence of music
- –a silenced voice (political) or our choice to be silent about certain subjects
- –the silence of the audience (and/or critical silence) or the silence of God: that no one will answer us back
- –the silence of our own effort or our own voice—how to begin writing

These silences have a relationship to one another. They have roots in the silences possible (or enforced) in the body itself. We can know about them by thinking about the physical body itself (not the mind, not the mouth, not the senses, but the whole body as we have it) as Sappho referred to it, "a speaking instrument."[1]

Helen Keller with only three senses still managed a more sensory prose than most writers with five:[2]

Suddenly a change passed over the tree. All the sun's warmth left the air. I knew the sky was black, because all the heat, which meant light to me, had died out of the atmosphere. A strange odour came up from the earth. I knew it, it was the odour that always precedes a thunderstorm, and a nameless fear clutched at my heart. I felt absolutely alone, cut off from my friends and the firm earth. The immense, the unknown, enfolded me. I remained still and expectant; a chilling terror crept over me. I longed for my teacher's return; but above all things I wanted to get down from that tree.

Keller herself has been silenced by history—she is known most widely as a child who learned to read and write despite her handicaps; what she did with that education is conveniently ignored: it's not good politics when your pick-yourself-up-by-your-bootstraps poster girl becomes a member of the International Workers of the World and a tireless labor and antiwar activist.

Like Keller, for whom writing was kinesthetic, about the surface of her hand and the ridges of the paper, Agnes Martin painted great and mostly white canvases. They are not to be compared to Rauschenberg's white canvases nor Ryman's. They were each concerned with the quality of white or blankness, with the texture of surface. Martin's canvases only happened to be white because she was working in the subtlest gradations of experience.

She claimed the simplest of motives and she herself lived in years (during the late sixties and early seventies) in silence. Her late and greatest paintings have such innocuous titles as "Love," "Happiness," and "A Pleasant Evening."

Martin, formerly a resident of New York City and interested in creating paintings with geometric and vertical forms, had (like O'Keeffe before her) a revelation of the blankness and horizon of the desert when she visited New Mexico. She moved there and never returned to the city.

Her canvases themselves that she turned sideways to work on the paint grain would fall with gravity the correct way to create the essence of the horizontal.

"The future's a blank page," Martin reasoned. "I used to look in my mind for the unwritten page/if my mind was empty enough I could see it."[3]

The body has silent spaces inside. Sound resonates through these spaces. The body requires vibration (of the heart for one thing) to continue its existence. That all matter vibrates is a pretty thought but it is borne out by the hardest of hard sciences as well. Quantum physics tells us how the building blocks of the universe exist and what they do is vibrate. Or put another way, as Gertrude Stein explained it, "Always from the beginning there was to me all living as repeating."[4]

What about poetry that would dare to drop everything, to just drift, to load the spaces up with that silence:

Susan Howe: "Leap-frogging the Middle Ages/I see you and
  you see I see you."[5]

Howe is interested also in silenced and suppressed voices and
histories—the fraught and wartorn landscape of what would be-
come (after ethnic cleansing) bucolic New England, the voice of
Jonathan Swift's mistress Stella, Charles Peirce's mistress Juliet,
and so on.

So we (teachers of any sacred language—Sanskrit, Arabic,
Latin—will all concur) actually invoke magical powers of vowels
and consonants when we pronounce poems.

As when Dennis Lee asks, "When schist prevails, and squa-
mous/pinpricks of appetite/vamp to a second future—who'll
chant the/mutant genesis? Who celebrate/an aevum cleansed
of us?"[6]

The modulations between the short vowel sounds and the
various labials, fricatives, liquids, etc., give actual shape to en-
ergy through the body.

P, B: expulsion. lips
L, R, M, N: liquid. Tongue.
S, Z: sibilant
G, C, K, Q: hard sound. throat.
D, T: the teeth
F, V, W: breath through the teeth and/or lip
H: breath
J, Y: tongue and breath. Nearly a vowel

Dennis Lee knows that the mouth is terrain and the alphabet
a set of geological forces brought to bear upon it:[7]

Song sinister. Song
ligature:
sing *counter.*
Are there honks, are there glyphs, are there
bare alingual grunts that
tonguefastly cleave to the iflift of
habitat mending? The judder of unsung un-
sung?

These energetic spaces for sound can be filled by sounds coming from the outside into the body (spaces of the ear) from the inside of the body moving up and out (chest and throat for most people but for yogis or opera singers and the like can go from the pelvis to the top of the head).

In the ancient science of yoga we learn there are seven energy centers in the body. They lie along the spine. Each had an associated syllable meant to charge and energize that place, release the various energy forces and channels that travel the body (in yoga science there are 72,000, but three main channels, the largest that runs the length of the spinal column and two others that spiral around it in the shape of a helix of DNA—every place they cross from the base of the pelvis to the crown of the head there is a chakra).

The one syllable you may all know from yoga is the syllable AUM said to be the sound of the universe itself. This word has four components which each vibrate at a different frequency from heart to crown of head.

Chant AUM with hand at heart   ("A" emphasizes)
Then at throat   ("U" emphasizes)
Then at top of head   ("M" emphasizes)

"A" at heart center: emotions, vulnerability, openness, how others treat you

"U" at throat center: expression, speech, how you treat others

"M" at the crown: intellect, spiritual growth, reflection, relation with teachers

Then of course there is the silence that follows.

This is the part of the poem no one can complete. When you pray God is not going to answer you. When you write a poem you are always lonely. There is something reifying and essential to the act of creation in this loneliness. I think Dickinson knew it and Melville too. Lest we get too esoteric in our thinking, imagine Mahmoud Darwish's plight when he received his permission papers to return to Palestinian territories after twenty-four years of denial. Never mind that Ramallah, where he received permission to go, wasn't his home and that he still wasn't allowed to go to Galilee where his family and mother still lived and leave aside just for a moment that he never thought much of the Oslo Accords (though masterfully restrained himself from saying I told you so), and let's instead reflect for a moment on his real concern: "Questions, like poisoned arrows, rained down on you: 'What will you write about when you haven't got exile? What will you write about when you haven't got the Occupation? Exile is existence. The existing Occupation is what hampers the effectiveness of the imagination. I will write better. But why are questions like these not put to other peoples? Is it because the necessary condition for Palestinian creativity is bondage?'"[8]

In the first place Darwish was asked to be silent about the injustices done to the Palestinian civil population; indeed he was jailed several times when he refused to comply. In the second place, after he became a representative voice of his people, he was asked to be silent about his personal life (his accounts of his Israeli lover were taken as allegorical) and focus only on political struggle. After his return to Ramallah his first collection was called *The Stranger's Bed* and mostly dealt with this love affair. Arab critics were not amused.

The individual human body, the one you have right now, tender, resonating and echoing with the sounds you make every day when you speak, is the one that is subject to these laws of nation and empire, the one that has to have its proper papers, proper sexual practice, proper gender.

Heteronormativity and the structures of global capital that both define it and require it for continued sustenance may be equally considered the enemies of both poetry and of the sound-based body.

For this reason I take to poets who can return me to basic sounds, vowels and consonants that resonate and reconstruct a human reality.

It puts me in mind of the closing of Jane Cooper's sequence "The Weather of Six Mornings":[9]

Rest.
        A violin bow, a breeze

        just touches the birches.
        Cheep! a new flute

        tunes up in a birch top.
        A chipmunk's warning skirrs

        Whose foot disturbs these twigs?
        To the sea of received silence

        why should I sign
        my name?

What's resting in the line can be the poem itself, all creation, or that violin bow. A bow at rest on a string is preparing to make music or has it just completed it? Either way the music's silence resonates like the breeze, the baby bird in the tree, the chipmunk. After all the animal speech—a noisy poem after all—the presence of a human foot on twigs seems unbearable and unnecessary, leading to the stunning final question. What reason, then, Cooper asks, to add anything at all to the silent sound of creation?

But that stunning question of Cooper's made more magnificent by its publication as the closing poem of her first collection is not meant to be rhetorical but real. She does not leave it hanging in space, but spends a career at the liminal edge of silence negotiating the relationship between an individual and corporeal existence and the fact of creation. The poetry may seem spiritual, but it is precisely the border between the tangible body and the ineffable nature of the spirit that Cooper seeks to know and understand.

Silent spaces in a poem reveal the surface of what is in sound of course. Music depends on its modulations.

Hazrat Inayat Khan, the musician and Sufi teacher, explains that the physical property of all matter in the universe is vibrations, that is to say: sound: "Man is not only formed of vibrations, but he lives and moves in them; they surround him as the fish is surrounded by water; and he contains them within him as the tank contains water."[10]

For a moment we listen to the way the world quivers.

Look: at the trees outside, the leaves. That this is what all matter is doing, what your hand is doing, then pen and paper.

Vinyasa, with breath.

Cage, *4'33"*

Music depends on its modulations and irregularities:

Cage, *Ryoanji* (both string and horn versions)

When we sing these sounds in our body, when we listen to the silence we are taking our bodies and body's perceptual awareness to the "frontiers" of what we know.

And of course as Cage taught us, there isn't silence. Within the silent spaces is an immensity of energetic activity of various emotional tonalities:

Chandra, *ABONECRONEDRONE 6*
Ono, *Cambridge 1969* (original version from *Unfinished Music 2*)

Bhanu Kapil devised a set of questions to move into the area of personal silences, the places we will not "break." One of these questions runs: "Tell me the one thing you have never spoken about to anyone, not even to the person you have spent your whole life loving."

Go ahead, answer.

The body in silence is a receptive thing. You can hear the external world and also the internal sounds. It vibrates through blood and breath. When I studied with Broumas she had us (as is practiced in Zen monasteries and other kinds as well) practice ritual silence. Communication then was by gesture only and emotional expressivity.

The body that knows its sounds and silences increases its power and ability to speak in the face of the growing injustice and technology that works to supplant the functions of the body.

So perhaps we seek new paths, new ways of seeing the page and the poem—

In place of a conclusion, I offer the first half of a syllabus for a semester-long class on silence and sound.

Notes

1. Bernard, *Sappho,* 8.
2. Keller, 13.
3. Martin, 38.
4. Stein, 103.
5. Susan Howe, 66.
6. Lee, 3.
7. Lee, 67.
8. Darwish, *Abesnt Presence,* 97.
9. Cooper, 63.
10. Khan, 5.

Syllabus for a Semester on Silence

Week 1:

Silent meditation five minutes.

Look: at paintings of Agnes Martin. Look: at a dance by Kazuo Ohno

Write: A poem using physical silence on the page. The poem can use up to 20 words only (repeated words will count twice) but should occupy the entire space of the page. Explore how the empty space can be sculptural. Take a look how different writers have used the space of the page: *Cascadia*, Brenda Hillman, *Commons*, Myung Mi Kim, *The View They Arrange*, Dale Going, *Afterrimages*, Joan Retallack

Week 2:

Silent meditation, seven minutes.

Listen to Sheila Chandra's *ABoneCroneDrone* sequence

Write: A poem using limited vocabulary—twenty words maximum—which can be of any length or combination. Distribute between nouns, verbs and other parts of speech carefully. The poems should repeat and recombine phrases with musical intent. Some strategies can include puns, homonyms (multiple homonyms can be used as a single word), and words that double in multiple parts of speech.

Week 3:

Silent meditation, ten minutes

Listen: Alice Coltrane, *Universal Consciousness*

Read: poem, "Home. Deep. Blue." by Jean Valentine

Write: A poem in which the language stutters and disappears at the end. Say something with your silence.

Week 4:
Silent meditation fifteen minutes.
Chant: A, U, M and AUM to tune resonances inside the body.
Write: Take a poem you have completed on any subject of your choosing. Then take out all the consonants of the poem. Perform the poem for workshop using only the vowel sounds. We will workshop the poem as normal, discussing its emotional texture, musical rhythm, prosody, etc.

Week 5:
Meditation for thirty minutes and chanting as above.
Reading: Last section of *Zong!* By NourBese Philip, "Silence Wager Stories" by Susan Howe and "River Antes" by Myung Mi Kim
Write: A poem on a subject you have always avoided in your writing (from your own experience) in which the suppressed or silenced part of your story or narrative appears in half-tone either in the margins or beneath/within the text of your poem. You may also use "strike-through" or other strategy to indicate a suppressed or silenced voice.

Week 6:
Meditation for thirty minutes and chanting as above
Reading: *Sappho's Gymnasium,* by Olga Broumas
Group Chanting: Group AUM—the class chants AUM together, as each person ends and begins again the sound of AUM will go one, passed between us and unending.
Revision exercise: Write poems on your own body. Prepare your portfolio for the class by revising each poem with your hands on your own body. Recite the various poems with your hands on your lower belly, solar plexus, heart center, throat, third eye and crown of the head. Revise vowels and consonants to the tune of the body and its silences.

Week 7:
Silent meditation all week. Do not speak. For the remainder of the semester, do not write on paper. Write in your mind.

The Opening

I heard it told that the Prophet once told about how all of the Quran is contained in this chapter; that the whole of this chapter was contained in its first line; that the whole of its first line was contained in its first phrase; the whole of its first phrase contained in its first letter; that the whole of its first letter (*beh*) was contained in the dot beneath it. The miracle of a book being contained in the physical space of a dot the size of a period is of course no longer a miracle.

The idea of infinite verses unfolding from a single phrase *Bismillah* is enticing in the extreme. It means the most complex ideas progress from the simple but it also means that you cannot understand the simplest phrase about divinity without reading hundreds upon hundreds of verses expounding it. One has to read the entire book, in other words, in order to understand even the first sentence of it, even the first phrase of it. Even, in fact, the first letter of it.

The first line, *bismillah-hir-rahman-nir-raheem,* does not disappear. Though it counts as a numbered line in the very first chapter of the Quran, it opens all subsequent chapters, though not as a numbered line. In this way, the first chapter, Al-Fateha, the Opening, is invoked throughout the Quran. A single chapter, Repentence (Al-Ta'uba), opens without it, but another chapter, the one that tells of the relationship between Solomon and Bilqis, the Queen of Sheba, contains two repetitions of the phrase.

The line resounds with untranslatability. In the first case the word "Allah" does not really mean "God." The word, both as it is written and as it is pronounced in Arabic, is a contraction for "Al-Ilaha." An "ilah" is something that is worshiped, a "god." In fact, in some places in the Quran (for example in Surat-al-Nas, Mankind), Allah is referred to as the "ilah-hin-nas," the "god of men." To say "Al-Ilaha" is to speak of the unity and singleness of the creative force of the universe. To speak it as its code or contraction, "Allah," or to write the Arabic word itself, is somewhat akin to writing the words "YHWH" or "G-d."

The words "Rahman" and "Raheem" are both qualities of G-d, in Arabic innately related to each other in both sound and appearance. Rahman is usually translated as "beneficent" or "compassionate"—it's that quality of G-d that is magnanimous, that loves all creation no matter what its activity or thought. It is the thought of G-d independent and beyond activity and cause and effect. "Raheem" is usually translated as "merciful"—it's that quality of G-d which is forgiving; a quality of G-d that is connected to human existence and activity and cause and effect. Through the coupling of these two concepts that generally (though not always) appear side by side, G-d is at once intimately involved with and completely removed from the human causal world.

Or perhaps we should speak of plural "worlds," which is how the chapter speaks of them. This plurality and infinity within the incomprehensible unity of the divine is one of the paradoxes whose answer may be found in the ancient Sanskrit text, the Siva Samhita, which tells us, "As in innumerable cups full of water, many reflections of the sun are seen, but the substance is the same; similarly individuals, like cups, are innumerable, but the vivifying spirit, like the sun, is one. As in a dream the one soul creates many objects by mere willing, but on awaking everything vanishes but the one soul; so is this universe" (Siva Samhita, I:35–36).

Both like and unlike Vedanta philosophy, in Islam, existence or being has an endpoint, and this moment, the *yawm-id-deen*, or Day of Judgment, is also mentioned in this verse. In an endless twist between plurality and unity, infinity and absolute ending, the supplicant asks to be kept on the right path and not the path of those who go astray. Certainly everyone is on a path and, by extension of the metaphor, faith and the practice of such is a journey.

In Arabic the brief chapter is rhythmically sublime, its vowels opening out into sound and end-stopped rhyme, its consonants sonically stunning. It's easy to imagine it as the rolling waves of itself echoing through all the lines and chapters of the Quran that follow it, echoing its themes and sounds over and over again.

It's a chapter that's legendarily associated with many miracles—curing of the sick, raising of the dead.

Perhaps it is true that it contains the entire book, true that it contains even itself in its first line, in its first phrase, in its first letter. That first letter, *beh*, is the not-really-distant ancestor of our "B." The letter itself, closer of the word "alphabet," has constant associations; in most languages it appears, both in its semic form and semantic meaning, with the concept for "home," and, specifically in the Hebrew Roman, and Arabic letters, with the shape of a tent or shelter or house.

I suppose the dot beneath the swoop is the human who lives inside.

Bibliography

Adnan, Etel. *In the Heart of the Heart of Another Country,* San Francisco: City Lights, 2005.

Alexander, Meena. *Poetics of Dislocation,* Ann Arbor, MI: University of Michigan Press, 2009.

Alexander, Meena. *Quickly Changing River.* Chicago, IL: Northwestern University Press, 2008.

Ali, Agha Shahid. *The Veiled Suite.* New York: Norton, 2009.

Ali, Kazim. *The Far Mosque,* Farmington, ME: Alice James, 2005.

Ali, Kazim. *The Fortieth Day,* Rochester, NY: BOA, 2008.

Ali Kazim. *The Disappearance of Seth,* Wilkes-Barre, PA: Etruscan, 2009.

Ali Kazim. *Bright Felon: Autobiography and Cities,* Middletown, CT: Wesleyan University Press, 2009.

Back, Rachel Tzvia. *Azimuth,* Riverdale, NY: Sheep Meadow, 2001

Bearhart, Bryan. 2011. In *American Ghost: Poets on Life After Industry,* ed. Lillien Waller, Ithaca, NY: Stockport Flats.

Bernard, Mary. *Sappho.* Berkeley, CA: University of California Press, 1986.

Bey, Hakim. *T.A.Z. The Temporary Autonomous Zone, Ontological Anarchy, Poetic Terrorism,* Brooklyn, NY: Autonomedia, 2003.

Bitsui, Sherwin. *Flood Song,* Port Townsend, WA: Copper Canyon, 2009.

Broumas, Olga. *Rave: Poems 1975–1999.* Port Townsend, WA: Copper Canyon, 1999.

Broumas, Olga, and T. Begley. *Sappho's Gymnasium.* Port Townsend, WA: Copper Canyon, 1994.

Carson, Anne. *Grief Lessons: Four Plays by Euripides.* New York: New York Review of Books, 2006.

Clifton, Lucille, *The Collected Poems of Lucille Clifton,* Rochester, NY: BOA, 2013.

Conoley, Gillian. *Lovers in the Used World.* Pittsburgh, PA: Carnegie Mellon Press, 2001.

Cooper, Jane. *The Flashboat: Poems New and Reclaimed.* New York: W.W. Norton, 2000.

Critical Art Ensemble, *The Flesh Machine: Cyborgs, Designer Babies and New Eugenic Consciousness.* Brooklyn, NY: Autonomedia, 1998.

Darwish, Mahmoud. (Mounir Akash, translator). *The Adam of Two Edens,* Syracuse, NY: Syracuse University Press, 2001.

Darwish, Mahmoud. (Mohammed Shaheen, translator). *Absent Presence.* London, UK: Hesperus, 2010.

Darwish, Mahmoud. (Sinan Antoon, translator). *In the Presence of Absence.* Brooklyn, NY: Arpichelago Books, 2011.

Darwish, Mahmoud. (Ibrahim Muhawi, translator). *Memory for Forgetfulness.* Berkeley, CA: University of California Press, 1995.

Diaz, Natalie. *When My Brother Was an Aztec,* Port Townsend: Copper Canyon, 2012.

Dickman, Michael. *Flies.* Port Townsend, WA: Copper Canyon, 2011.

Duncan, Robert. *Letters,* Chicago, IL: Flood Editions, 2008.

Fitzgerald, Robert. *The Odyssey of Homer.* New York: Vintage Classics, 1990.

Foo, Josey and Leah Stein. *A Lily Lilies.* Callicoon, NY: Nightboat Books, 2011.

Goldsmith, *Uncreative Writing.* New York: Columbia University Press. 2011.

Graham, *The End of Beauty.* New York: Ecco Press. 1987.

Graham, *Dream of the Unified Field.* New York: Ecco Press. 1993.

Graham, *Swarm.* New York: Ecco Press. 2000.

Kuusisto, *Eavesdropping.* New York: WW Norton. 2006.

Haraway, Donna. *Simians, Cyborgs and Women: The Reinvention of Nature.* New York: Routledge, 1991.

Hoskote, Ranjit. *I, Lalla: The Poems of Lal Ded.* Delhi: Penguin India, 2011.

Howe, Fanny. *Selected Poems,* Berkeley, CA: University of California Press, 2000.

Howe, Susan. *Souls of the Labadie Tract,* New York: New Directions, 2007.

Jordan, June. *Directed by Desire: Collected Poems.* Port Townsend, WA: Copper Canyon, 2007.

Kapil, Bhanu. *Schizophrene.* Callicoon, NY: Nightboat Books, 2011.

Keller, Helen. *The Story of My Life,* Mineola, NY: Dover Thrift Editions, 1996.

Khan, Hazrat Inayat. *The Music of Life.* Rhinebeck, NY: Omega Publications, 1983.

Lalla. (Coleman Barks, translator). *Naked Song.* Athens, GA: Maypop Press, 1992.

Lee, Dennis. *Testament.* Toronto: House of Anansi Press, 2012.